Human Rights

Series Editor: Cara Acred

Volume 300

061250

THE HENLEY COLLEGE LIBRARY

Independence Educational Publishers

First published by Independence Educational Publishers

The Studio, High Green

Great Shelford

Cambridge CB22 5EG

England

© Independence 2016

Copyright

Photocopy licence

ISBN-13: 978 1 86168 741 8

Printed in Great Britain
Zenith Print Group

Contents

Introduction

Human Rights is Volume 300 in the **ISSUES** series. The aim of the series is to offer current, diverse information about important issues in our world, from a UK perspective.

ABOUT HUMAN RIGHTS

In 2015, at least 122 countries tortured or ill-treated people worldwide. Despite our ever-socially-evolving world, human rights violations remain consistently abhorrent. This book features articles from organisations such as Liberty, Girls Not Brides and Amnesty International, alongside many others – exploring issues such as child marriage, torture and FGM. It also looks at human rights law in the UK, internationally and within Europe. This includes examination of the Human Rights Act, the UN Convention on the Rights of the Child, anti-slavery laws and the European Convention on Human Rights.

OUR SOURCES

Titles in the **ISSUES** series are designed to function as educational resource books, providing a balanced overview of a specific subject.

The information in our books is comprised of facts, articles and opinions from many different sources, including:

⇨ Newspaper reports and opinion pieces

⇨ Website factsheets

⇨ Magazine and journal articles

⇨ Statistics and surveys

⇨ Government reports

⇨ Literature from special interest groups.

A NOTE ON CRITICAL EVALUATION

Because the information reprinted here is from a number of different sources, readers should bear in mind the origin of the text and whether the source is likely to have a particular bias when presenting information (or when conducting their research). It is hoped that, as you read about the many aspects of the issues explored in this book, you will critically evaluate the information presented.

It is important that you decide whether you are being presented with facts or opinions. Does the writer give a biased or unbiased report? If an opinion is being expressed, do you agree with the writer? Is there potential bias to the 'facts' or statistics behind an article?

ASSIGNMENTS

In the back of this book, you will find a selection of assignments designed to help you engage with the articles you have been reading and to explore your own opinions. Some tasks will take longer than others and there is a mixture of design, writing and research-based activities that you can complete alone or in a group.

FURTHER RESEARCH

At the end of each article we have listed its source and a website that you can visit if you would like to conduct your own research. Please remember to critically evaluate any sources that you consult and consider whether the information you are viewing is accurate and unbiased.

Useful weblinks

www.50forfreedom.org

www.amnesty.org

blogs.unicef

www.bowgroup.org

www.care.org.uk

www.childrenengland.org

www.theconversation.com

www.crae.org.uk

www.girlsnotbrides.org

www.theguardian.com

www.heraldscotland.com

www.huffingtonpost.co.uk

www.independent.co.uk

www.liberty-human-rights.org.uk

www.nationalcrimeagency.gov.uk

www.racecard.org

www.un.org

www.unodc.org

What are human rights?

Human rights belong to every member of the human family regardless of sex, race, nationality, socio-economic group, political opinion, sexual orientation or any other status.

Human rights are universal. They apply to all people simply on the basis of being human.

Human rights are inalienable. They cannot be taken away simply because we do not like the person seeking to exercise their rights. They can only be limited in certain tightly-defined circumstances and some rights, such as the prohibition on torture and slavery, can never be limited.

Human rights are indivisible. You cannot pick and choose which rights you want to honour. Many rights depend on each other to be meaningful – so, for example, the right to fair trial would be meaningless without the prohibition on discrimination,

and the right to free speech must go hand in hand with the right to assemble peacefully.

Human rights are owed by the State to the people – this means public bodies must respect your human rights and the Government must ensure there are laws in place so that other people respect your human rights too. For example, the right to life requires not only that the actions of those working on behalf of the State do not lead to your death, but that laws are also in place to protect you from the actions of others that might want to do you harm.

Human rights were first recognised internationally by the Universal Declaration on Human Rights in 1948. This was quickly followed by the adoption, two years later, of the European Convention on Human Rights. In 1998 the Human Rights Act was passed, making the rights and freedoms in the

European Convention on Human Rights directly enforceable in the UK. It entered into force on 2 October 2000.

The UK is also a party to a number of other international instruments that seek to protect and promote other human rights.

International human rights

The Universal Declaration of Human Rights

In 1948, in the aftermath of the Second World War, the newly formed United Nations adopted the Universal Declaration of Human Rights (UDHR). In response to the atrocities committed before and during the War, the international community sought to define the rights and freedoms necessary to secure the dignity and worth of each individual.

The European Convention on Human Rights and the Council of Europe

In Europe, another newly formed international body, the Council of Europe, set about giving effect to the UDHR in a European context. The resulting European Convention on Human Rights was signed in 1950 and ratified by the United Kingdom, one of the first countries to do so, in 1951.

At the time there were only ten members of the Council of Europe (the countries subscribed to the Convention), and all were Western European. The Council has since expanded, particularly following the collapse of the communist states in Eastern Europe. Now 47 member countries subscribe to the European Convention.

Over the years a number of additional Protocols to the Convention have been adopted. Only some of these confer new rights. The United Kingdom has ratified some but not all of these substantive Protocols.

Other international human rights instruments

Over the years, a number of other international human instruments giving effect to the UDHR have been drafted and adopted. Some of these are truly international, e.g. the International Covenant on Civil and Political Rights, while others are regional, e.g. the American Convention on Human Rights and the African Charter on Human and Peoples' Rights. Some deal with specific issues, e.g. the Convention against Torture, and some with the rights of specific groups, e.g. the Refugee Convention and the Convention on the Rights of the Child. The United Kingdom has ratified many of these international conventions.

The European Court of Human Rights and enforcement of the European Convention

The European Convention system was unusual in that, very early on, a court was set up to interpret and ensure compliance with the Convention. The European Court of Human Rights was established in 1959 and the United Kingdom has allowed an individual right of application to the Court since 1966. Before applying to the Court, applicants are required to pursue any legal proceedings in this country that are capable of giving them redress for the violation of their Convention rights. Now that the Human Rights Act is in force, this will usually involve pursuing a claim under the Act.

Enforcement of other international instruments

The example of a regional human rights court has been followed under both the Inter-American and African systems. Other international human rights systems have established committees to which complaints of breaches can be made, provided the relevant government allows. Apart from the European Convention, the only international human rights instrument under which the United Kingdom permits an individual right of complaint is the Convention on the Elimination of all Forms of Discrimination against Women (CEDAW).

Some international instruments require participating states to report regularly on what they are doing to ensure compliance. Groups such as Liberty often participate in these reporting cycles by commenting on their government's report, or by producing a shadow report.

International human rights instruments in British law

The Human Rights Act was passed in 1998 in order to 'give further effect' to the European Convention in British law. Under the Act, public authorities in this country are now required to act in a way that respects people's rights under the Convention, and people can now rely on their Convention rights in legal proceedings.

This is not the case with the other international human rights instruments that the United Kingdom has ratified. While people can refer to these in proceedings before the British courts, the courts will not directly apply them. They may still have some effect for two reasons:

⇨ Where there is some ambiguity as to what the law requires, the courts will assume that the law should be interpreted in a way that complies with the United Kingdom's international obligations;

⇨ In interpreting the rights under the European Convention, the courts here, but more particularly the European Court of Human Rights, will have regard to other international human rights instruments.

⇨ The above information is reprinted with kind permission from Liberty. Please visit www.liberty-human-rights.org.uk for further information.

In 2015...

122 or more countries tortured or otherwise ill-treated people

30 or more countries illegally forced refugees to return to countries where they would be in danger

War crimes or other violations of the 'laws of war' were carried out in at least 19 countries

Source: Amnesty International Report 2015/16

What is human trafficking?

Human trafficking involves recruiting, transporting or holding a person by use of threats, coercion or deception in order to exploit them. Essentially, it is the oppression and abuse of people motivated by financial or personal gain. It is often described as a form of modern day slavery.

> Mary fled her village in Nigeria because of abuse from the community elders. Whilst living on the streets of the capital city she met a man called Tony who told her she could get a good job in England. He bought her a ticket and came with her to London. Hours after she arrived, Mary was taken to a brothel where she was locked in a room. For many months she was forced to have sex with up to ten or 12 men a day who paid money to Tony.

Trafficking happens all over the world, across international borders and within countries. In the UK each year about 2,000 men, women and children are helped to escape from trafficking, but this is just the tip of the iceberg. The Government estimates there are 10,000 – 13,000 victims of modern slavery in the UK.

Victims of trafficking are often tricked into coming to the UK by false promises or because of threats against them or their family. People are trafficked into prostitution, pornography, agricultural and building labour, manufacturing, domestic servitude, forced begging, benefit fraud, petty criminality and organ removal. They are forced to work for little or no pay; they may have limited freedom and poor living conditions. Many experience physical or emotional abuse.

How can I respond?

You can stay informed about what the Government is doing by signing up to our *Loose the Chains* e-mails: care.org.uk/loosethechains-signup

You can write to your MP and your MSPs, AMs or MLAs or arrange to meet them in person, either alone or with other supporters. Our *Loose the Chains* e-mails will highlight specific opportunities to do so.

You can contact your Police and Crime Commissioner (in England and Wales) to encourage them to make trafficking a key priority in your area.

You can speak about this issue to people that you know. Contact your local newspaper, or speak at your church, school or student groups. You can join with people in your area to campaign together.

You can be watchful for signs of trafficking and keep your eyes open for it in your community. Understand the signs at: modernslavery.co.uk

> Bien is a child from Vietnam. When his mother fell ill, the family needed to take a loan out to cover the cost of her healthcare. In return, Bien was told that he needed to come to the UK to work off the loan. On his arrival Bien was initially forced to work as a domestic servant but later was moved to a cannabis factory, where he cultivated plants day and night. Bien was arrested after police raided the factory, and although eventually recognised as a victim of trafficking Bien disappeared from care and is presumed to be back in the hand of his traffickers.

If you suspect an instance of trafficking in your area you can contact:

⇨ the Police (101 or 999 if someone is in immediate danger)

⇨ Crimestoppers (0800 555 111 crimestoppers-uk.org) where you can leave information anonymously

Do not confront a suspected trafficker or victim of trafficking. Your safety and that of any possible victims is of primary importance.

March 2016

⇨ The above information is reprinted with kind permission from CARE. Please visit www.care.org.uk for further information.

Types of human trafficking

There are several broad categories of exploitation linked to human trafficking:

Sexual exploitation

Sexual exploitation involves any non-consensual or abusive sexual acts performed without a victim's permission. This includes prostitution, escort work and pornography. Women, men and children of both sexes can be victims. Many will have been deceived with promises of a better life and then controlled through violence and abuse.

Forced labour

Forced labour involves victims being compelled to work very long hours, often in hard conditions, and to hand over the majority if not all of their wages to their traffickers. Forced labour crucially implies the use of coercion and lack of freedom or choice for the victim. In many cases, victims are subjected to verbal threats or violence to achieve compliance.

Manufacturing, entertainment, travel, farming and construction industries have been found to use forced labour by victims of human trafficking to some extent. There has been a marked increase in reported numbers in recent years.

Often large numbers of people are housed in single dwellings and there is evidence of 'hot bunking', where a returning shift takes up the sleeping accommodation of those starting the next shift.

The International Labour Organization [ILO] has identified six elements which individually or collectively can indicate forced labour. These are:

⇨ Threats or actual physical harm

⇨ Restriction of movement and confinement to the workplace or to a limited area

⇨ Debt-bondage

⇨ Withholding of wages or excessive wage reductions that violate previously made agreements

⇨ Retention of passports and identity documents (the workers can neither leave nor prove their identity status)

⇨ Threat of denunciation to the authorities where the worker is of illegal status.

Domestic servitude

Domestic servitude involves the victim being forced to work in private households. Their movement will often be restricted and they will be forced to perform household tasks such as child care and house-keeping over long hours and for little if any pay. Victims will lead very isolated lives and have little or no unsupervised freedom. Their own privacy and comfort will be minimal, often sleeping on a mattress on the floor in an open part of the house.

In rare circumstances where victims receive a wage, it will be heavily reduced, as they are charged for food and accommodation.

Organ harvesting

Organ harvesting involves trafficking people in order to use their internal organs for transplant. The illegal trade is dominated by kidneys, which are in the greatest demand. These are the only major organs that can be wholly transplanted with relatively few risks to the life of the donor.

Child trafficking

Children are particularly vulnerable to exploitation by individual traffickers and organised crime groups. They can be deliberately targeted by crime groups, or ruthlessly exploited by the people who should protect them. About a quarter of the victims referred to the UK Human Trafficking Centre are children.

Common countries of origin include Vietnam, Nigeria, Romania, Slovakia and the UK.

⇨ The above information is reprinted with kind permission from the National Crime Agency. Please visit www.nationalcrimeagency. gov.uk for further information.

Human trafficking indicators

Not all the indicators listed below are present in all situations involving trafficking in humans. Although the presence or absence of any of the indicators neither proves nor disproves that human trafficking is taking place, their presence should lead to investigation.

Victims of trafficking in humans can be found in a variety of situations. You can play a role in identifying such victims.

General indicators

People who have been trafficked may:

⇨ Believe that they must work against their will

⇨ Be unable to leave their work environment

⇨ Show signs that their movements are being controlled

⇨ Feel that they cannot leave

⇨ Show fear or anxiety

⇨ Be subjected to violence or threats of violence against themselves or against their family members and loved ones

⇨ Suffer injuries that appear to be the result of an assault

⇨ Suffer injuries or impairments typical of certain jobs or control measures

⇨ Suffer injuries that appear to be the result of the application of control measures

⇨ Be distrustful of the authorities

⇨ Be threatened with being handed over to the authorities

⇨ Be afraid of revealing their immigration status

⇨ Not be in possession of their passports or other travel or identity documents, as those documents are being held by someone else

⇨ Have false identity or travel documents

⇨ Be found in or connected to a type of location likely to be used for exploiting people

⇨ Be unfamiliar with the local language

⇨ Not know their home or work address

⇨ Allow others to speak for them when addressed directly

⇨ Act as if they were instructed by someone else

⇨ Be forced to work under certain conditions

⇨ Be disciplined through punishment

⇨ Be unable to negotiate working conditions

⇨ Receive little or no payment

⇨ Have no access to their earnings

⇨ Work excessively long hours over long periods

⇨ Not have any days off

⇨ Live in poor or substandard accommodations

⇨ Have no access to medical care

⇨ Have limited or no social interaction

⇨ Have limited contact with their families or with people outside of their immediate environment

⇨ Be unable to communicate freely with others

⇨ Be under the perception that they are bonded by debt

⇨ Be in a situation of dependence

⇨ Come from a place known to be a source of human trafficking

⇨ Have had the fees for their transport to the country of destination paid for by facilitators, whom they must pay back by working or providing services in the destination

⇨ Have acted on the basis of false promises.

Children

Children who have been trafficked may:

⇨ Have no access to their parents or guardians

⇨ Look intimidated and behave in a way that does not correspond with behaviour typical of children their age

⇨ Have no friends of their own age outside of work

⇨ Have no access to education

⇨ Have no time for playing

⇨ Live apart from other children and in substandard accommodations

⇨ Eat apart from other members of the 'family'

⇨ Be given only leftovers to eat

⇨ Be engaged in work that is not suitable for children

⇨ Travel unaccompanied by adults

⇨ Travel in groups with persons who are not relatives.

The following might also indicate that children have been trafficked:

⇨ The presence of child-sized clothing typically worn for doing manual or sex work

⇨ The presence of toys, beds and children's clothing in inappropriate places such as brothels and factories

⇨ The claim made by an adult that he or she has 'found' an unaccompanied child

⇨ The finding of unaccompanied children carrying telephone numbers for calling taxis

⇨ The discovery of cases involving illegal adoption.

Domestic servitude

People who have been trafficked for the purpose of domestic servitude may:

⇨ Live with a family

⇨ Not eat with the rest of the family

- ⇨ Have no private space
- ⇨ Sleep in a shared or inappropriate space
- ⇨ Be reported missing by their employer even though they are still living in their employer's house
- ⇨ Never or rarely leave the house for social reasons
- ⇨ Never leave the house without their employer
- ⇨ Be given only leftovers to eat
- ⇨ Be subjected to insults, abuse, threats or violence.

Sexual exploitation

People who have been trafficked for the purpose of sexual exploitation may:

- ⇨ Be of any age, although the age may vary according to the location and the market
- ⇨ Move from one brothel to the next or work in various locations
- ⇨ Be escorted whenever they go to and return from work and other outside activities
- ⇨ Have tattoos or other marks indicating 'ownership' by their exploiters
- ⇨ Work long hours or have few if any days off
- ⇨ Sleep where they work
- ⇨ Live or travel in a group, sometimes with other women who do not speak the same language
- ⇨ Have very few items of clothing
- ⇨ Have clothes that are mostly the kind typically worn for doing sex work
- ⇨ Only know how to say sex-related words in the local language or in the language of the client group
- ⇨ Have no cash of their own
- ⇨ Be unable to show an identity document.

The following might also indicate that children have been trafficked:

- ⇨ There is evidence that suspected victims have had unprotected and/or violent sex

- ⇨ There is evidence that suspected victims cannot refuse unprotected and/or violent sex
- ⇨ There is evidence that a person has been bought and sold
- ⇨ There is evidence that groups of women are under the control of others
- ⇨ Advertisements are placed for brothels or similar places offering the services of women of a particular ethnicity or nationality
- ⇨ It is reported that sex workers provide services to a clientele of a particular ethnicity or nationality
- ⇨ It is reported by clients that sex workers do not smile.

Labour exploitation

People who have been trafficked for the purpose of labour exploitation are typically made to work in sectors such as the following: agriculture, construction, entertainment, service industry and manufacturing (in sweatshops).

People who have been trafficked for labour exploitation may:

- ⇨ Live in groups in the same place where they work and leave those premises infrequently, if at all
- ⇨ Live in degraded, unsuitable places, such as in agricultural or industrial buildings
- ⇨ Not be dressed adequately for the work they do: for example, they may lack protective equipment or warm clothing
- ⇨ Be given only leftovers to eat
- ⇨ Have no access to their earnings
- ⇨ Have no labour contract
- ⇨ Work excessively long hours
- ⇨ Depend on their employer for a number of services, including work, transportation and accommodation
- ⇨ Have no choice of accommodation
- ⇨ Never leave the work premises without their employer
- ⇨ Be unable to move freely

- ⇨ Be subject to security measures designed to keep them on the work premises
- ⇨ Be disciplined through fines
- ⇨ Be subjected to insults, abuse, threats or violence
- ⇨ Lack basic training and professional licences.

The following might also indicate that people have been trafficked for labour exploitation:

- ⇨ Notices have been posted in languages other than the local language
- ⇨ There are no health and safety notices
- ⇨ The employer or manager is unable to show the documents required for employing workers from other countries
- ⇨ The employer or manager is unable to show records of wages paid to workers
- ⇨ The health and safety equipment is of poor quality or is missing
- ⇨ Equipment is designed or has been modified so that it can be operated by children
- ⇨ There is evidence that labour laws are being breached
- ⇨ There is evidence that workers must pay for tools, food or accommodation or that those costs are being deducted from their wages.

Begging and petty crime

People who have been trafficked for the purpose of begging or committing petty crimes may:

- ⇨ Be children, elderly persons or disabled migrants who tend to beg in public places and on public transport
- ⇨ Be children carrying and/or selling illicit drugs
- ⇨ Have physical impairments that appear to be the result of mutilation
- ⇨ Be children of the same nationality or ethnicity who move in large groups with only a few adults

- ⇨ Be unaccompanied minors who have been 'found' by an adult of the same nationality or ethnicity

- ⇨ Move in groups while travelling on public transport: for example, they may walk up and down the length of trains

- ⇨ Participate in the activities of organised criminal gangs

- ⇨ Be part of large groups of children who have the same adult guardian

- ⇨ Be punished if they do not collect or steal enough

- ⇨ Live with members of their gang

- ⇨ Travel with members of their gang to the country of destination

- ⇨ Live, as gang members, with adults who are not their parents

- ⇨ Move daily in large groups and over considerable distances.

The following might also indicate that people have been trafficked for begging or for committing petty crimes:

- ⇨ New forms of gang-related crime appear

- ⇨ There is evidence that the group of suspected victims has moved, over a period of time, through a number of countries

- ⇨ There is evidence that suspected victims have been involved in begging or in committing petty crimes in another country.

- ⇨ The above information is reprinted with kind permission from the United Nations Office on Drugs and Crime. Please visit www.unodc.org for further information.

Trafficking in children on the increase, according to latest UNODC Report

The 2014 *Global Report on Trafficking in Persons* released today in Vienna and in various UNODC field office locations across the world shows that one in three known victims of human trafficking is a child – a five per cent increase compared to the 2007–2010 period. Girls make up two out of every three child victims, and together with women, account for 70 per cent of overall trafficking victims worldwide.

"Unfortunately, the report shows there is no place in the world where children, women and men are safe from human trafficking," said UNODC Executive Director Yury Fedotov. "Official data reported to UNODC by national authorities represent only what has been detected. It is very clear that the scale of modern-day slavery is far worse."

No country is immune – there are at least 152 countries of origin and 124 countries of destination affected by trafficking in persons, and over 510 trafficking flows criss-crossing the world. Trafficking mostly occurs within national borders or within the same region, with transcontinental trafficking mainly affecting rich countries.

In some regions – such as Africa and the Middle East – child trafficking is a major concern, with children constituting 62 per cent of victims.

Trafficking for forced labour – including in the manufacturing and construction sectors, domestic work and textile production – has also increased steadily in the past five years. About 35 per cent of the detected victims of trafficking for forced labour are female.

There are, however, regional variations: victims in Europe and Central Asia are mostly trafficked for sexual exploitation, whereas in East Asia and the Pacific forced labour drives the market. In the Americas, the two types are detected in almost equal measure.

Most trafficking flows are interregional, and more than six out of ten victims have been trafficked across at least one national border. The vast majority of convicted traffickers – 72 per cent – are male and citizens of the country in which they operate.

The report highlights that impunity remains a serious problem: 40 per cent of countries recorded few or no convictions, and over the past ten years there has been no discernible increase in the global criminal justice response to this crime, leaving a significant portion of the population vulnerable to offenders.

"Even if most countries criminalise trafficking, many people live in countries with laws which are not in compliance with international standards that would afford them full protection, such as the Trafficking in Persons Protocol." Mr. Fedotov said.

"This needs to change," added Mr Fedotov. "Every country needs to adopt the UN Convention against Transnational Organised Crime and the protocol and commit themselves to the full implementation of their provisions."

24 November 2014

- ⇨ The above information is reprinted with kind permission from the United Nations Office on Drugs and Crime. Please visit www.unodc.org for further information.

Common myths about human trafficking

1. Human trafficking and people smuggling are the same thing

There are important differences between human trafficking and people smuggling. The main difference is the element of exploitation. People being smuggled as illegal migrants have usually consented to being smuggled. Trafficking victims have not consented, or have been tricked into consent.

What happens to each of them at the end of their journey will also be very different. The relationship between an illegal migrant and a people smuggler is a commercial transaction which ends on completion of the journey. However, for people who are trafficked, the purpose of the journey is to put them somewhere where they can be exploited for the sake of the traffickers' profits. The journey is only the beginning.

It can nevertheless be difficult to distinguish between trafficking and smuggling scenarios for many reasons, including:

⇨ People who begin as smuggled migrants may become victims of trafficking, i.e. there is a change of circumstances at some point during the process

⇨ The same people acting as traffickers may also act as smugglers and use the same routes for both trafficking and smuggling

⇨ Conditions for smuggled persons may be so bad that it is difficult to believe that they consented to it.

2. You cannot be a victim of trafficking if you gave your consent to be moved

Someone becomes a victim of trafficking not because of the journey they make but because of the exploitation they experience at the end of that journey.

Any consent they give to make the journey in the first place is likely to have been gained fraudulently, for example with the promise of a job or a better standard of living.

This is why the Palermo Protocol makes clear that human trafficking is about the three elements of movement, control and exploitation.

3. Trafficking only affects people from other countries

Whilst people smuggling always involves illegal border crossing and entry into another country, human trafficking for exploitation can happen within someone's own country, including Britain.

4. Many trafficked women are already prostitutes

This is a common misconception. The majority of trafficking victims working as prostitutes will have been forced into it against their will. They have often been trafficked without their consent, deceived into consenting to the journey, or deceived about the kind of work they would be doing at the end of the journey.

⇨ The above information is reprinted with kind permission from the National Crime Agency. Please visit www.nationalcrimeagency.gov.uk for further information.

© Crown copyright 2016

Claimed exploitation type	Female	Male	Trans-sexual	Unknown	Total 2015	2014–2015 % change
Adult – domestic servitude	292	61	0	0	353	50.9%
Adult – labour exploitation	161	734	0	0	895	53.3%
Adult – organ harvesting	1	1	0	0	2	100.0%
Adult – sexual exploitation	813	48	2	0	863	28.2%
Adult – unknown exploitation	98	73	0	0	171	-3.4%
Minor – domestic servitude	44	25	0	0	69	-2.8%
Minor – labour exploitation	21	267	0	0	288	39.8%
Minor – organ harvesting	0	3	0	0	3	200.0%
Minor – sexual exploitation (non-UK national)	89	23	0	0	112	20.4%
Minor – sexual exploitation (UK national)	95	10	0	0	105	64.1%
Minor – unknown exploitation type	130	273	0	2	405	71.6%
Total	**1,744**	**1,518**	**2**	**2**	**3,266**	**–**

Source: National Referral Mechanism Statistics, End of Year Summary, 2015, National Crime Agency

Modern slavery and human trafficking: myths and facts

Modern slavery is all around us, but most people don't even realise it. Learn the truth about these common myths and then sign up to end modern slavery for good.

Myth: slavery is a thing of the past

Fact: no, it is not. Slavery has ancient roots in history and still exists today in many different forms. Human trafficking, bonded labour and forced domestic work are just a few examples. But that doesn't mean it's inevitable. A coordinated effort by governments and activists around the world could end modern slavery for good. That's what the ILO's Protocol on Forced Labour is all about.

Myth: relatively few people are victims of modern slavery

Fact: there are more people in slavery today than at any other time in history. There are over 21 million children, women and men living in modern slavery, three out of every 1,000 people worldwide. If they all lived together in a single city, it would be one of the biggest cities in the world.

Sources:

2012 *Global Estimate of Forced Labour*

United Nations Department of Economic and Social Affairs: *World Urbanization Prospects*

Myth: modern slavery only happens in the developing world.

Fact: modern slavery happens everywhere. There are over 1.5 million people working in slavery-like conditions in Europe, North America, Japan and Australia.

Source:

2012 Global Estimate of Forced Labour

Myth: sex trafficking accounts for most cases of modern slavery

Fact: most of the people in slavery work in industries such as agriculture, fishing, construction, manufacturing, mining, utilities and domestic work. Around one in five are victims of sexual exploitation.

Myth: modern slavery isn't a big money-maker

Fact: modern slavery is huge business. A recent ILO study estimated that modern slavery generates annual profits of over US$150 billion, which is as much as the combined profits of the four most profitable companies in the world.

Sources:

Profits and Poverty: The Economics of Forced Labour, ILO (2014)

Fortune Global 500

Myth: modern slavery doesn't affect me

Fact: modern slavery affects everyone.

Even if you're not a victim of modern slavery, you're still affected by it. Businesses, for example, face unfair competition from unscrupulous companies who reap the profits of modern slavery. That may put pressure on them to lower wages or cut benefits. Meanwhile, governments lose out on precious tax revenue while facing huge legal costs from prosecuting modern-slavery cases – money which could be spent on public services like education, healthcare or public transportation.

Myth: most of the money from modern slavery is made in the developing world

Fact: the annual profits per victim of forced labour are far, far higher in developed economies and the European Union than they are anywhere else in the world.

Source:

Profits and Poverty: The Economics of Forced Labour, ILO (2014)

Myth: there isn't very much I can do to help people trapped in modern slavery

Fact: you can play a part in the fight to end slavery. It is up to governments to enact and enforce legislation, protect their citizens and ratify the Protocol on Forced Labour. And you can make sure that happens by showing you care:

⇨ Sign up to join the 50 for Freedom campaign.

⇨ Ask at least two of your friends to sign up too.

⇨ Ask your representative to support the Protocol on Forced Labour.

⇨ The above information is reprinted with kind permission from the International Labour Organization. Please visit www.50forfreedom.org for further information.

© International Labour Organization 2016

Child marriage

Every year 15 million girls are married as children, denied their rights to health, education and opportunity, and robbed of their childhood. If we do nothing, by 2030 an estimated 16.5 Million girls a year will marry as children.

Each year, 15 million girls are married before the age of 18. That is 28 girls every minute – married off too soon, endangering their personal development and well being. With more young people on our planet than ever before, child marriage is a human rights violation that we must end to achieve a fairer future for all.

Child brides are often disempowered, dependent on their husbands and deprived of their fundamental rights to health, education and safety. Neither physically nor emotionally ready to become wives and mothers, child brides are at greater risk of experiencing dangerous complications in pregnancy and childbirth, becoming infected with HIV/AIDS and suffering domestic violence. With little access to education and economic opportunities, they and their families are more likely to live in poverty.

Nations also feel the impact: a system that undervalues the contribution of young women limits its own possibilities. In this way, child marriage drains countries of the innovation and potential that would enable them to thrive.

A persistent problem

Child marriage persists across countries, fuelled by poverty, social and cultural norms. For many families, it is a perceived economic need – one less mouth to feed. Long-held beliefs and traditions based on gender inequality mean that becoming a wife and mother is often deemed a daughter's only choice.

Child marriage facts

⇨ More than 700 million women alive today were married before their 18th birthday. That is the equivalent of 10% of the world's population.

⇨ If there is no reduction in child marriage, an additional 1.2 Billion girls will be married by 2050.

⇨ Some child brides are as young as eight or nine.

⇨ Most adolescent pregnancies (90%) take place within marriage.

⇨ Pregnancy and childbirth complications are among the leading causes of death in girls aged 15 to 19 in low- and middle-income countries.

Compelling reasons to act now

Globally, the rates of child marriage are slowly declining. Growing commitments to address the issue, such as the inclusion of target 5.3 To end child, early and forced marriage in the sustainable development goals, are encouraging. However, there are urgent reasons to double our efforts.

It violates human rights and is illegal

In many countries, child marriage is prohibited, but existing laws are often not enforced or provide exceptions for parental consent or traditional and customary laws. Child marriage reinforces gender inequality and violates human rights. Tolerating any injustice makes it easier for others to exist.

It perpetuates poverty

Married girls often leave school and so can lack the skills to help lift their families out of poverty. Without addressing child marriage, the international community will fail to achieve its commitment in the sustainable development goals to reduce global poverty.

The longer we wait, the bigger the problem will be

Millions of girls and women already suffer the consequences of child marriage. If we do nothing, population growth means that, by 2050, the total number of women married as children will grow to 1.2 Billion, with devastating

consequences for girls, their families and their countries. Boys are also affected – 33 million men today were married before the age of 15 and 156 million before the age of 18.

Progress is possible

The complex mix of cultural and economic factors mean there is not a single, simple solution. But, through partnership, long-term programming and a willingness to learn from our successes and failures, we can end child marriage in a generation.

Why does child marriage happen?

Tradition

Child marriage is a traditional practice that in many places happens simply because it has happened for generations – and straying from tradition could mean exclusion from the community. But as Graça Machel, widow of Nelson Mandela, says, traditions are made by people – we can change them.

Gender roles

In many communities where child marriage is practised, girls are not valued as much as boys – they are seen as a burden. The challenge will be to change parents' attitudes and emphasise that girls who avoid early marriage and stay in school will likely be able to make a greater contribution to their family and their community in the long term.

Poverty

Where poverty is acute, giving a daughter in marriage allows parents to reduce family expenses by ensuring they have one less person to feed, clothe and educate. In communities where a dowry or 'bride price' is paid, it is often welcome income for poor families; in those where the bride's family pay the groom a dowry, they often have to pay less money if the bride is young and uneducated.

Security

Many parents marry off their daughters young because they feel it is in her best interest, often to ensure her safety in areas where girls are at high risk of physical or sexual assault.

Global pressure

Girls not brides shows the will of a global movement to end child marriage. By connecting and amplifying the voice of civil society organisations across the world, we help instil the global pressure that makes ground-level change happen.

⇨ The above information is reprinted with kind permission from Girls Not Brides. Please visit www.girlsnotbrides.org for further information.

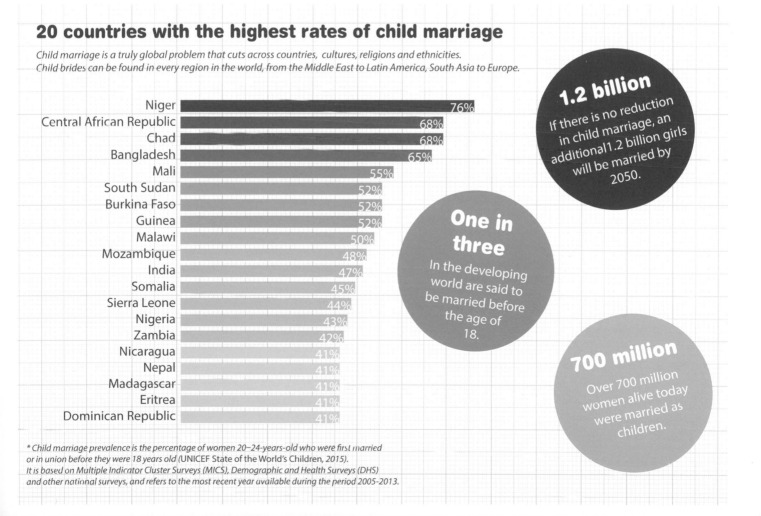

20 countries with the highest rates of child marriage

Child marriage is a truly global problem that cuts across countries, cultures, religions and ethnicities.
Child brides can be found in every region in the world, from the Middle East to Latin America, South Asia to Europe.

Country	%
Niger	76%
Central African Republic	68%
Chad	68%
Bangladesh	65%
Mali	55%
South Sudan	52%
Burkina Faso	52%
Guinea	52%
Malawi	50%
Mozambique	48%
India	47%
Somalia	45%
Sierra Leone	44%
Nigeria	43%
Zambia	42%
Nicaragua	41%
Nepal	41%
Madagascar	41%
Eritrea	41%
Dominican Republic	41%

1.2 billion
If there is no reduction in child marriage, an additional 1.2 billion girls will be married by 2050.

One in three
In the developing world are said to be married before the age of 18.

700 million
Over 700 million women alive today were married as children.

* Child marriage prevalence is the percentage of women 20–24-years-old who were first married or in union before they were 18 years old (UNICEF State of the World's Children, 2015). It is based on Multiple Indicator Cluster Surveys (MICS), Demographic and Health Surveys (DHS) and other national surveys, and refers to the most recent year available during the period 2005-2013.

NHS records more than 1,000 FGM cases in just three months

By Sarah Ann Harris

More than 1,000 cases of female genital mutilation (FGM) were recorded in just three months in the UK, it has been revealed.

For the quarter April to June 2015, there were 1,036 newly-recorded cases of FGM in England, with a total of 1,159 attendances for FGM, according to the Press Association.

Nine of the individuals were aged under 18 when they were first seen, the data from the Health and Social Care Information Centre (HSCIC) revealed.

The shocking figures have been made public after the health service began recording incidences of FGM for the very first time.

Much of the FGM reported may be historic, as the abuse is normally carried out on infants and young teenagers. The NHS data did not specify whether it was carried out in the UK or abroad, as is the case in many instances of FGM.

Tanya Barron, chief executive of global children's charity Plan UK, which works to combat FGM worldwide, said: "It's shocking to see the extent of FGM here in the UK.

"We've seen hugely increased attention on this problem in the past few years and we are now waking up to the scale of this terrible practice.

"What we must always keep in mind though is that this is not specifically a British problem.

"FGM is a practice with an inherently global dimension.

"And while it's vital that we do everything we can to stop FGM here in the UK, as well as to support the girls and women affected by it, the reality is that this practice won't end in the UK until it is ended worldwide."

FGM is illegal in the UK. It is also illegal to take a female abroad for the purposes of FGM.

The maximum jail term for carrying out or enabling FGM is 14 years.

According to the World Health Organisation (WHO), FGM is carried out for social and religious reasons and is an "extreme form of discrimination against women".

Babies born to women who have undergone FGM suffer a higher rate of death compared with those born to women who have not undergone the procedure.

Women with FGM also have increased risk of stillbirth, infants that need resuscitation and low birth weight babies.

FGM is estimated to lead to an extra one or two baby deaths per 100 deliveries worldwide.

An estimated 130 million women and girls around the world are through to be living with FGM.

An international day of zero tolerance of FGM took place earlier this year, with a number of measures, including NHS recording, outlined to help to end the horrifying practice.

This included better training for frontline health workers on how to communicate with patients about the highly sensitive issue, allowing clinicians to note on a child's health record if they are at risk of FGM and an additional £2 million for a programme backed by Barnardo's and the Local Government Association to create a specialised team of social workers.

23 September 2015

⇨ The above information is reprinted with kind permission from The Huffington Post UK. Please visit www.huffingtonpost.co.uk for further information.

Forced marriage: at the intersection of risk, identity and policy

By Heather Harvey

The issue of forced marriage, a little like female genital mutilation and honour crimes, means victims of such practices can find themselves caught at the heart of political rhetoric on race, crime, immigration and gender, whilst obviously also needing a service often of life-or-death significance.

In June 2012 the Prime Minister announced that forcing someone into a marriage would become a criminal offence in England and Wales from May 2014. This decision follows a number of Home Affairs Committee Inquiries and consultations on forced marriage over the years (2005, 2008, 2011) and in particular into whether or not it should be made criminal.

The fact that there have been repeated inquiries and consultations on criminalisation reflects the very complex and powerful arguments both in favour of criminalisation and against it. A gut instinct would suggest that of course forced marriage should be criminal and that it would be culturally relativist for it not to be treated this seriously. It's a human rights abuse. It can incur a range of harms for both men and for women. It can involve intense emotional and sometimes physical pressure amounting to abuse. It can cause lasting mental health problems, it can sometimes involve physical assault, false imprisonment and kidnap. For young women, in addition, it can have serious effects on her opportunities for education, employment, financial independence and personal and social life. In addition, young women may be subjected to rape and to attacks on her right to sexual and reproductive autonomy. There is, therefore, an inherent and persuasive logic to the criminalisation of forced marriage. Other arguments in favour suggest

that criminalisation may have a deterrent effect, would send out a very strong message and could empower both victims and public sector to have the confidence to challenge and resist it.

Many, but not all, women's groups working with women victims of forced marriage, however, have argued against its criminalisation. Their arguments principally cluster around concerns that such a measure has not been adequately thought through or factored in the practical consequences when it comes to trying to help a young person who is at risk of a forced marriage. They are concerned that parents would still do it anyway but more discreetly by taking young girls abroad to isolate them from help. They fear that girls would not seek help as they would fear getting their parents in trouble and they fear that some girls may be lulled into a false sense of security. Girls may think that because forced marriage is criminal they are safe and so would not plan an exit strategy or confront their parents putting themselves at further risk. This divergence of views results in a very clear call for Government to set in place effective monitoring and tracking of cases to identify what the practical implications of their measure will be so that they can respond accordingly.

Some other opponents of criminalising forced marriage question the motives of government for their intense focus on this issue and their eagerness to legislate. They highlight that the offences involved in bringing about a forced marriage are often already criminal (kidnap, false imprisonment, rape etc.) They add that this is a measure that would have disproportionate impact on certain segments of the population who already may feel scrutinised, feared, stereotyped and marginalised. (The majority of

reported cases to date have been from South Asian communities and some African backgrounds.) They also stress that many of the measures proposed to address forced marriage focus heavily on enforcement-type approaches such as criminalisation or on immigration responses, like raising the age of sponsoring for marriage, increasing the probation period etc. Given that the Foreign Office itself recognises that the motives and drivers for forced marriage are multiple, complex and varied; this concentration on immigration measures causes critics to question the Government's motives.

The political football at the heart of all this is the victims who are navigating their multiple identities of race, gender and religion and not uncommonly, sexuality and disability as well. Foreign and Commonwealth Office (FCO) statistics indicate that they may receive around 1,500 phone calls a year from a variety of sources for help with forced marriage. Between 82 and 85% of cases referred to them are female. The majority of cases recorded reflect UK demographics of settled second - and third-generation immigration with a heavy proportion being families originating from Pakistan, Bangladesh and India. Their youngest reported case was aged two years, their eldest 71 years. A significant proportion are young adolescents and the majority are aged between 18 and 25. Where the information was recorded, 114 cases involved victims with disabilities and 22 identified as LGBT.

Eaves[1], a charity working on all forms of violence against women and girls, received a small amount of funding from FCO which enabled us to undertake a research project.

---

1 Eaves closed in November 2015.

The research aimed to identify young people's views:

⇨ On forced marriage,

⇨ On government's responses to it – notably criminalisation,

⇨ On their understanding of the gendered nature of the issue,

⇨ On what they see as the causes and motivations for the practice and what they would like to recommend in solution.

Some of the most interesting findings of this research relate to the gender dynamics of forced marriage. There is a recognition that it is hard for boys to ask for help for this issue due to feeling embarrassed as a male to come forward as a victim when most services are targeted at women. Interestingly, participants' gut reactions showed that they were far from certain that forced marriage was different for men and for women. Similarities included that the pressure brought to bear on young people was predominantly emotional and that the mental health impact of forced marriage was very severe for both men and women. Some women showed very high empathy with male suffering seeing it as worse for men because they related to men's sense of 'masculinity': "Men aren't supposed to be pushed around like that." Whereas they showed a high tolerance and

normalisation of female suffering: "Women have to accept abuse as part of their lot." However, it soon became apparent that participants could identify a more gendered pattern to the harms, including rape, forced childbirth and the cessation or contraction of education, employment, financial independence and personal life for females.

They also identified that for men forced into marriage they may go through with it: "It's an easy option to say yes" because they could continue their education and employment and either may try for a divorce or may be able to live a personal life outside the marriage. A particularly concerning finding, however, was that 85% of survey respondents agreed with the fact that it may be hard for a man to resist a forced marriage because he himself may be expected to be an enforcer for his siblings. One young woman highlighted this by stressing that women would rarely turn to their brothers for help as their brothers were often part of the problem. This poses a major dilemma for policy makers who need both to target help at young men at risk but also to recognise and challenge the dual role of boys both as victims and perpetrators.

Another gender variation was that participants were able to recognise that parents may, albeit unconsciously, use different and

specifically gendered strategies to persuade boys or girls into a marriage. They highlighted that girls may come under pressure for bringing shame and dishonour on the family and for being selfish. Parents might appeal to young men more on the basis of their role as a man, an adult, a standard setter and an enforcer: "It's the same but what is used might be sometimes a bit different – to get men is like 'You are the man of the family, you have to' – the sense of responsibility and grown up adulthood so he feels older and responsible whereas with women's it's 'You don't know how it will make us feel.' Again, this suggests that more work could be helpful for men to understand how their sense of machismo is manipulated against them. More generally it was remarkable that considering these interviews and surveys drew out major gendered differentials, only one survey respondent (of 101) and one interviewee specifically framed the issue as one of gender discrimination and the two women who referenced feminism apologised for doing so!

On the issue of criminalisation, many of the above arguments were rehearsed. There was 98% support for criminalisation in principle but considerable disquiet as to how it would work in practice, leading many to call for close monitoring and tracking of the actual outcomes. One interviewee in particular took issue with the criminalisation approach and contextualised this as racism and Islamophobia: "I think that's rubbish man – it's just wrong – it's just trying to make trouble for us." In the interviews, there was something of a gender split with young men being much more likely to oppose criminalisation: "It's a family thing, you can't interfere" and "You're not going to want to chat all that in public." The young men were also much less likely to expect or want any third party intervention. They were more likely to put the onus on the victim to resist the pressure and to feel it unfair to blame the parents if the victim just gave in: "But if it's you that can't stand up to the nagging and begging and

UM... DO WE BOTH HAVE THE SAME PROBLEMS WITH THIS?

guilt then is it fair to blame the parents for that?" This may reflect something of a macho culture but it also demonstrated that young men need to be supported to realise that giving into such pressure is not weakness but natural and is a parental abuse of power that they can and should be able to ask for help against. A common finding was that while the theoretical distinction of choice and consent between forced and arranged marriage is well known, the reality of it is that young people found it extremely hard to identify where emotional pressure was 'force'.

Another factor that emerged was that the culture of respect for one's elders and the belief that they know what's right and do the best for you is powerful and makes it difficult for young people to challenge the practice. This was particularly so with young women who were more likely to perceive their parent's motives as benign, which could be an additional factor in their susceptibility to emotional pressure. This led to some participants stressing that it is not fair or effective to place the burden of challenging such practices on the young people themselves.

We are grateful to have a chance to discuss this research with the readers of *Race Card*. All too often we are all in our various silos whereas in fact we have multiple facets to our identities and these can be affected by hidden or overt political agenda. The cohort for this research crossed youth, race, gender, religion and, to a lesser extent, disability and sexuality. Bringing our fields closer together can only enhance not just the research but the policy and practice initiatives that we advocate for in support of our service user groups.

5 February 2014

⇨ The above information is reprinted with kind permission from the Runnymede Trust. Please visit www.racecard.org. uk for further information.

Criminalising forced marriage has not helped its victims THE CONVERSATION

An article from The Conversation.

By Aisha K. Gill, Associate Professor in Criminology, University of Roehampton

In the year since forced marriage was criminalised in the UK, only one conviction has taken place. In June, a 34-year-old man was jailed for forcing a 25-year-old woman to marry him under duress. Merthyr Crown Court in Wales heard that the man – who was already married to someone else – repeatedly raped his victim over a period of months, threatened to publish footage of her having a shower and told her that her parents would be killed, unless she agreed to become his wife.

The defendant was put on the sex offenders' register and sentenced to 16 years in custody, to be released under an extended licence for another five years afterwards. This is an important case, which will raise questions about whether these offences – which also included rape, voyeurism and bigamy, alongside forced marriage – could have been prosecuted under the existing criminal law.

Before forced marriage was criminalised, the Forced Marriage (Civil Protection) Act 2007 enabled courts to issue protection orders against those who attempt or conspire to force someone into marriage. Between November 2008 (when the Act came into force) and September 2014, there were 762 applications filed for forced marriage protection orders. During this same period, 785 forced marriage protection orders were issued (some of which may have been interim orders, issued during other proceedings).

Last year, the Government's Forced Marriage Unit provided support and assistance for 1,267 possible cases of forced marriage. It is troubling, then, that there has been only one conviction since June last year under the 2014 Act.

An adversarial system

Laws are only effective when properly enforced. Those who believe the new sanctions will eradicate forced marriage overlook the fact that criminal prosecutions require a high standard of proof. This standard will have a dramatic effect on the rate of successful prosecutions.

Failed prosecutions, and cases that do not proceed to prosecution may result in victims being discredited or shamed within their family and community, while those at fault may feel exonerated. This raises the risk that victims will suffer isolation and further abuse, because their family and community are likely to ostracise them, or even seek revenge.

The adversarial British criminal justice system requires that victims and witnesses give evidence in court, and submit to being cross-examined. The rules of the court require that the prosecution must disclose all their evidence to the defence. This includes highly sensitive information gathered by the police, local authorities and other organisations when a complaint is made by a victim or information provided by a third party about a forced marriage.

If the case proceeds to court, the victim and any witnesses may, in some cases, face the sharing and discussion of this information in public. Apart from placing them at risk of harm, the impact of being made to participate in difficult, and often lengthy, public proceedings is likely to be significant. These practicalities demand further reflection from those who make the law.

Access to justice

Even if prosecution is successful, victims may still endure other challenges, and require extensive support from different services. For one thing, it's often the case that the victims of forced marriage, and those at risk, need assistance from specialist support services, in order to access justice in the first place.

Research by Rights of Women reveals that many victims of forced marriage cannot afford to pay for the legal assistance they require. For instance, foreign nationals may require immigration advice and assistance, while British citizens may need advice regarding family law remedies like marriage annulments, or contact with their children.

Cuts to Legal Aid have had a negative impact on victims' ability to obtain vital legal advice. As forced marriage cases are often extremely complex in a legal sense, it is crucial that advice is freely available to enable those in need to seek justice. And legal remedies are only one aspect of addressing forced marriage.

Legislation fails to address the day-to-day issues associated with protecting and supporting victims, and there have been no additional resources announced to meet these needs. This places the responsibility for supporting victims onto charities – particularly women's charities, since the vast majority of cases involve female victims.

The need for support

Rashida Manjoo – the UN's Special Rapporteur on violence against women – has called for the UK Government to "urgently evaluate the way women's support services are funded and then act to ensure a network of women-centred services are available to all who need them". In her report on violence against women in the UK, its causes and consequences – presented at the United Nations on 17 Jun 2015 – Manjoo points out that funding for these charities often falls short.

Evidence demonstrates that actual and potential victims of forced marriage are far more likely to approach and trust specialist black and minority ethnic women's services, rather than the state agencies. Yet few of these services currently receive adequate funding. And the limited resources available to local authorities often means that appropriate accommodation is all but non-existent. It is vital that these services are properly funded, even in times of austerity.

The situation is even more urgent for the 11% of victims who are under 16 years of age: they have little recourse to services, apart from overstretched and cash-strapped local authorities, many of whom are already overburdened with cases of child abuse and unable to provide appropriate accommodation.

The national shortage of suitable foster homes, and the lack of specialist carers with appropriate training in cultural sensitivity adds to the challenges faced by victims of forced marriage. This kind of training is urgently needed to ensure that criminal and civil support systems – including child protection services – are working effectively.

Ultimately, the success of the stand-alone law on forced marriage will depend on how effective it proves for victims. At present, too little consideration has been paid to the practicalities of this legislation, and its effect on victims themselves.

17 June 2015

⇨ The above information is reprinted with kind permission from *The Conversation*. Please visit www.theconversation.com for further information.

Global crisis on torture exposed by new worldwide campaign

Amnesty International has accused governments around the world of betraying their commitments to stamp out torture, three decades after the ground-breaking Convention Against Torture was adopted by the UN in 1984.

"Governments around the world are two-faced on torture – prohibiting it in law, but facilitating it in practice," said Salil Shetty, Amnesty International's Secretary General, as he launched Stop Torture, Amnesty International's latest global campaign to combat widespread torture and other ill-treatment in the modern world.

"Torture is not just alive and well – it is flourishing in many parts of the world. As more governments seek to justify torture in the name of national security, the steady progress made in this field over the last 30 years is being eroded."

Since 1984, 155 states have ratified the UN Convention Against Torture, 142 of which are researched by Amnesty International. In 2014, Amnesty International observed at least 79 of these still torturing – more than half the states party to the Convention that the organisation reports on. A further 40 UN states haven't adopted the Convention, although the global legal ban on torture binds them too.

Over the last five years, Amnesty International has reported on torture and other forms of ill-treatment in at least 141 countries from every region of the world – virtually every country in which it works. The secretive nature of torture means the true number of countries that torture is likely to be higher still.

In some of these countries torture is routine and systematic. In others, Amnesty International has only documented isolated and exceptional cases. The organisation finds even one case of torture or other ill-treatment totally unacceptable.

The Stop Torture campaign launches with a new media briefing, *Torture in 2014: 30 Years of Broken Promises*, which provides an overview of the use of torture in the world today.

The briefing details a variety of torture techniques – from stress positions and sleep deprivation to electrocution of the genitals – used against criminal suspects, security suspects, dissenting voices, political rivals and others.

As part of the campaign, Amnesty International commissioned a GlobeScan survey to gauge worldwide attitudes to torture. Alarmingly, the survey found nearly half (44%) of respondents – from 21 countries across every continent – fear they would be at risk of torture if taken into custody in their country.

The vast majority (82%) believe there should be clear laws against torture. However, more than a third (36%) still thought torture could be justified in certain circumstances.

"The results from this new global survey are startling, with nearly half of the people we surveyed feeling fearful and personally vulnerable to torture. The vast majority of people believe that there should be clear rules against torture, although more than a third still think that torture could be justified in certain circumstances. Overall, we can see broad global support amongst the public for action to prevent torture," said Caroline Holme, Director at GlobeScan.

Measures such as the criminalisation of torture in national legislation, opening detention centres to independent monitors, and video recording interrogations have all led to a decrease in the use of torture in those countries taking their commitments under the Convention Against Torture seriously.

Amnesty International is calling on governments to implement protective mechanisms to prevent and punish torture – such as proper medical examinations, prompt access to lawyers, independent checks on places of detention, independent and effective investigations of torture

allegations, the prosecution of suspects and proper redress for victims.

The organisation's global work against torture continues, but will focus in particular on five countries where torture is rife and Amnesty International believes it can achieve significant impact. Substantive reports with specific recommendations for each will form the spine of the campaign.

In Mexico, the Government argues that torture is the exception rather than the norm, but in reality abuse by police and security forces is widespread and goes unpunished. Miriam López Vargas, a 31-year-old mother of four, was abducted from her home town of Ensenada by two soldiers in plain clothes, and taken to a military barracks. She was held there for a week, raped three times, asphyxiated and electrocuted to force her to confess that she was involved in drug-related offences. Three years have passed, but none of her torturers have been brought to justice

Justice is out of reach for most torture survivors in the Philippines. A secret detention facility was recently discovered where police officers abused detainees 'for fun'. Police officers reportedly spun a 'wheel of torture' to decide how to torture prisoners. Media coverage led to an internal investigation and some officers being dismissed, but Amnesty International is calling for a thorough and impartial investigation which will lead to the prosecution in court of the officers involved. Most acts of police torture remain unreported and torture survivors continue to suffer in silence.

In Morocco and Western Sahara, authorities rarely investigate reports of torture. Spanish authorities extradited Ali Aarrass to Morocco despite fears he would be tortured. He was picked up by intelligence officers and taken to a secret detention centre, where he says they electrocuted his testicles, beat the soles of his feet and hanged him by his wrists for hours on end. He says the officers forced him to confess to assisting a terrorist group. Ali Aarass was convicted and sentenced to 12 years behind bars on the basis of that 'confession'. His allegation of torture has never been investigated.

In Nigeria, police and military personnel use torture as a matter of routine. When Moses Akatugba was arrested by soldiers he was 16 years old. He said they beat him and shot him in the hand. According to Moses he was then transferred to the police, who hanged him by his limbs for hours at a police station. Moses says he was tortured into signing a 'confession' that he was involved in a robbery. The allegation that he confessed as a result of torture was never fully investigated. In November 2013, after eight years waiting for a verdict, Moses was sentenced to death.

In Uzbekistan, torture is pervasive but few torturers are ever brought to justice. The country is closed to Amnesty International. Dilorom Abdukadirova spent five years in exile after security forces opened fire on a protest she was attending. On returning to Uzbekistan, she was detained, barred from seeing her family, and charged with attempting to overthrow the Government. During her trial, she looked emaciated with bruising on her face. Her family are convinced she had been tortured.

"30 years ago Amnesty led the campaign for a worldwide commitment to combat torture resulting in the UN's Convention Against Torture. Much progress has been made since, but it is disheartening that today we still need a worldwide campaign to ensure that those promises are fulfilled," said Salil Shetty.

13 May 2014

⇨ The above information is reprinted with kind permission from Amnesty International. Please visit www.amnesty.org for further information.

Five things you didn't know about female genital mutilation/cutting

More than 125 million women and girls in 29 countries in Africa and the Middle East have experienced Female Genital Mutilation or Cutting (FGM/C). UNICEF released a report on FGM/C last year that revealed some thought-provoking attitudes about the practice.

Here are five things about FGM/C that might surprise you:

1. **Boys and men state strong support for stopping the practice.** It's often presumed that men condone FGM/C and that it is one of the ways that they keep women subservient. This appears not to be the case. In fact, in countries such as Guinea, Sierra Leone and Chad, substantially more men than women want to see FGM/C end.

2. **Girls and women consistently underestimate the proportion of boys and men who want FGM/C to end.** In many countries, a large percentages of both women and men are unaware of what the opposite sex thinks about FGM/C.

3. **The majority of girls and women want FGM/C to end.** Girls' and women's attitudes about whether or not FGM/C should continue vary widely across the 29 countries where it is concentrated. However, in most of these countries, the majority thinks that FGM/C should end.

4. **The need to gain social acceptance is the most frequently stated reason for supporting the continuation of FGM/C.** Social acceptance trumps other reasons like better marriage prospects, preserving virginity, more sexual pleasure for the man, religious necessity and cleanliness/hygiene.

5. **Many girls who are cut have mothers who are against the practice.** Though a daughter's likelihood of being cut is much higher when her mother thinks the practice should continue, many cut girls have mothers who actually oppose FGM/C. Some mothers may thus have their daughters cut despite their personal feelings about the practice.

So what can we learn from these five points? First, more dialogue and communication is essential. Ways have to be found to make bring to the fore the 'hidden voices' that oppose FGM/C. Girls and women need to be empowered to speak out. Since substantial numbers of men and boys want the FGM/C to end, they can potentially be important agents of change and should be engaged in the conversation. There is clearly also a need for more open dialogue between men and women, and between boys and girls so that prevailing social expectations around FGM/C can be challenged.

A lot of progress had already been made in eliminating FGM/C. With continued effort and commitment many more girls can be spared the fate of their mothers and grandmothers.

11 February 2014

⇨ The above information is reprinted with kind permission from UNICEF. Please visit blogs.unicef.org for further information.

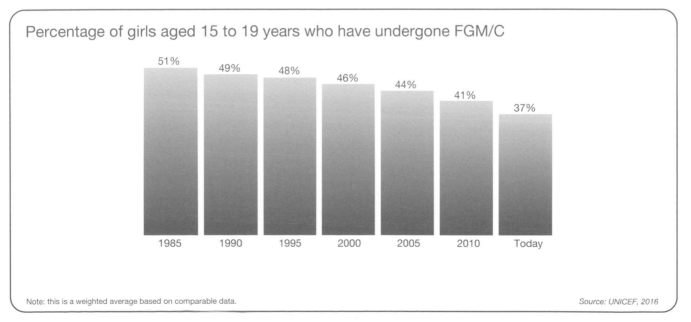

Percentage of girls aged 15 to 19 years who have undergone FGM/C

1985	1990	1995	2000	2005	2010	Today
51%	49%	48%	46%	44%	41%	37%

Note: this is a weighted average based on comparable data.

Source: UNICEF, 2016

Amnesty International Annual Report 2014/15

This has been a devastating year for those seeking to stand up for human rights and for those caught up in the suffering of war zones.

By Salil Shetty, Secretary General at Amnesty International

Governments pay lip service to the importance of protecting civilians. And yet the world's politicians have miserably failed to protect those in greatest need. Amnesty International believes that this can and must finally change.

International humanitarian law – the law that governs the conduct of armed conflict – could not be clearer. Attacks must never be directed against civilians. The principle of distinguishing between civilians and combatants is a fundamental safeguard for people caught up in the horrors of war.

And yet, time and again, civilians bore the brunt in conflict. In the year marking the 20th anniversary of the Rwandan genocide, politicians repeatedly trampled on the rules protecting civilians – or looked away from the deadly violations of these rules committed by others.

International failures

The UN Security Council had repeatedly failed to address the crisis in Syria in earlier years, when countless lives could still have been saved. That failure continued in 2014. In the past four years, more than 200,000 people have died – overwhelmingly civilians – and mostly in attacks by government forces. Around four million people from Syria are now refugees in other countries. More than 7.6 million are displaced inside Syria.

The Syria crisis is intertwined with that of its neighbour Iraq. The armed group calling itself Islamic State (IS, formerly ISIS), which has been responsible for war crimes in Syria, has carried out abductions, execution-style killings, and ethnic cleansing on a massive scale in northern Iraq. In parallel, Iraq's Shi'a militias abducted and killed scores of Sunni civilians, with the tacit support of the Iraqi Government.

The July assault on Gaza by Israeli forces caused the loss of 2,000 Palestinian lives. Yet again, the great majority of those – at least 1,500 – were civilians. The policy was, as Amnesty International argued in a detailed analysis, marked by callous indifference and involved war crimes. Hamas also committed war crimes by firing indiscriminate rockets into Israel causing six deaths.

Horrors of war

In Nigeria, the conflict in the north between government forces and the armed group Boko Haram burst onto the world's front pages with the abduction, by Boko Haram, of 276 schoolgirls in the town of Chibok, one of countless crimes committed by the group. Less noticed were horrific crimes committed by Nigerian security forces and those working with them against people believed to be members or supporters of Boko Haram, some of which were recorded on video, revealed by Amnesty International in August; bodies of the murdered victims were tossed into a mass grave.

In the Central African Republic, more than 5,000 died in sectarian violence despite the presence of international forces. The torture, rape and mass murder barely made a showing on the world's front pages. Yet again, the majority of those who died were civilians.

And in South Sudan – the world's newest state – tens of thousands of civilians were killed and two million fled their homes in the armed conflict between government and opposition forces. War crimes and crimes against humanity were committed on both sides.

Un veto

The above list – as this latest annual report on the state of human rights in 160 countries clearly shows – barely begins to scratch the surface. Some might argue that nothing can be done, that war has always been at the expense of the civilian population, and that nothing can ever change.

This is wrong. It is essential to confront violations against civilians, and to bring to justice those responsible. One obvious and practical step is waiting to be taken: Amnesty International has welcomed the proposal, now backed by around 40 governments, for the UN Security Council to adopt a code of conduct agreeing to voluntarily refrain from using the veto in a way which would block Security Council action in situations of genocide, war crimes and crimes against humanity.

That would be an important first step, and could save many lives.

The failures, however, have not just been in terms of preventing mass atrocities. Direct assistance has also been denied to the millions who have fled the violence that has engulfed their villages and towns.

More than words

Those governments who have been most eager to speak out loudly on the failures of other governments have shown themselves reluctant to step forward and provide the essential assistance that those refugees require – both in terms of financial assistance, and providing resettlement. Approximately 2% of refugees from Syria had been resettled by the end of 2014 – a figure which must at least triple in 2015.

Meanwhile, large numbers of refugees and migrants are losing their lives in the Mediterranean Sea as they try desperately to reach European shores. A lack of support by some EU Member States for search and rescue operations has contributed to the shocking death toll.

One step that could be taken to protect civilians in conflict would be to further restrict the use of explosive weapons in populated areas. This would have saved many lives in Ukraine, where Russian-backed separatists (despite unconvincing denials by Moscow of its involvement) and pro-Kyiv forces both targeted civilian neighbourhoods.

The importance of the rules on protection of civilians means that there must be true accountability and justice when these rules are violated. In that context, Amnesty International welcomes the decision by the UN Human Rights Council in Geneva to initiate an international inquiry into allegations of violations and abuses of human rights during the conflict in Sri Lanka, where in the last few months of the conflict in 2009, tens of thousands of civilians were killed. Amnesty International has campaigned for such an inquiry for the past five years. Without such accountability, we can never move forward.

Attacking the messenger

Other areas of human rights continued to require improvement. In Mexico, the enforced disappearance of 43 students in September was a recent tragic addition to the more than 22,000 people who have disappeared or gone missing in Mexico since 2006; most are believed to have been abducted by criminal gangs, but many are reported to have been subjected to enforced disappearance by police and military, sometimes acting in collusion with those gangs. The few victims whose remains have been found show signs of torture and other ill-treatment. The federal and state authorities have failed to investigate these crimes to establish the possible involvement of state agents and to ensure effective legal recourse for the victims, including their relatives. In addition to the lack of response, the Government has attempted to cover up the human

rights crisis and there have been high levels of impunity, corruption and further militarisation.

In 2014, governments in many parts of the world continued to crack down on NGOs and civil society – partly a perverse compliment to the importance of civil society's role. Russia increased its stranglehold with the chilling 'foreign agents law', language resonant of the Cold War. In Egypt, NGOs saw a severe crackdown, with use of the Mubarak-era Law on Associations to send a strong message that the government will not tolerate any dissent. Leading human rights organisations had to withdraw from the UN Human Rights Council's Universal Periodic Review of Egypt's human rights record because of fears of reprisals against them.

Courage

As has happened on many previous occasions, protesters showed courage despite threats and violence directed against them. In Hong Kong, tens of thousands defied official threats and faced down excessive and arbitrary use of force by police, in what became known as the 'umbrella movement', exercising their basic rights to freedoms of expression and assembly.

Human rights organisations are sometimes accused of being too ambitious in our dreams of creating change. But we must remember that extraordinary things are achievable. On 24 December, the international Arms Trade Treaty came into force, after the threshold of 50 ratifications was crossed three months earlier.

Amnesty International and others had campaigned for the treaty for 20 years. We were repeatedly told that such a treaty was unachievable. The treaty now exists, and will prohibit the sale of weapons to those who may use them to commit atrocities. It can thus play a crucial role in the years to come – when the question of implementation will be key.

Hope ahead

2014 marked 30 years since the adoption of the UN Convention against Torture – another

Convention for which Amnesty International campaigned for many years, and one reason why the organisation was awarded the Nobel Peace Prize in 1977.

This anniversary was in one respect a moment to celebrate – but also a moment to note that torture remains rife around the world, a reason why Amnesty International launched its global Stop Torture campaign this year.

This anti-torture message gained special resonance following the publication of a US Senate report in December, which demonstrated a readiness to condone torture in the years after the 11 September 2001 attacks on the USA. It was striking that some of those responsible for the criminal acts of torture seemed still to believe that they had nothing to be ashamed of.

From Washington to Damascus, from Abuja to Colombo, government leaders have justified horrific human rights violations by talking of the need to keep the country 'safe'. In reality, the opposite is the case. Such violations are one important reason why we live in such a dangerous world today. There can be no security without human rights.

We have repeatedly seen that, even at times that seem bleak for human rights – and perhaps especially at such times – it is possible to create remarkable change.

We must hope that, looking backward to 2014 in the years to come, what we lived through in 2014 will be seen as a nadir – an ultimate low point – from which we rose up and created a better future.

⇨ The above information is reprinted with kind permission from Amnesty International. Please visit www.amnesty.org for further information.

Cancelled UK deal won't change Saudi Arabia's appalling human rights record

An article from The Conversation.

THE CONVERSATION

By Rosa Freedman, Senior Lecturer (Law), University of Birmingham

Saudi Arabia's criminal justice system – if you can call it that – has suddenly started to attract increased international scrutiny. Reports of the crucifixion sentence for a teenage protester and the planned lashing of Karl Andree, a British grandfather caught with a few bottles of homemade wine, have been deeply unflattering for a state that likes to keep its domestic human rights record off the agenda.

Saudi Arabia is, for once, being excoriated in headlines around the world. And despite protestations to the contrary, it seems likely that those headlines might have had some impact on the UK Government's withdrawal from a prison consultancy bid worth almost £6 million.

Cancelling that deal is all very well, but it shouldn't take a death sentence for a British national for the UK to act. Saudi Arabia, as is well known, is a gross and systematic abuser of human rights. As with many other countries that deny fundamental rights to their citizens, it shields itself from global scrutiny not by improving its

performance, but keeping those violations under wraps.

Saudi Arabia is also very keen to wield its influence on the world stage, especially in the wake of the Iranian nuclear deal, which it regards as a serious security threat. It's precisely for that reason that we should pay attention to the way it treats its own citizens – and in particular, to the criminal sanctions it imposes upon anyone under its jurisdiction.

Home and away

Saudi Arabia's hallmark is the radical dissonance between its global aspirations and its domestic and regional behaviour. It clearly has its eyes on positions of prestige at the UN, and it cultivates an image as a regional powerhouse involved in 'solving' local conflicts (in Yemen, say), all while simultaneously striking a deeply protective posture on its domestic and international responsibilities.

This year alone, Saudi Arabia has sought the presidency of the United Nations Human Rights Council (a move that was blocked

through diplomatic means) and has taken its own military and political initiatives in Yemen and Syria.

Meanwhile, despite its vast wealth, the country apparently failed to welcome refugees fleeing conflicts in the region. Rights to adequate housing, food, water, healthcare and a livelihood are neither protected nor upheld. And it has been roundly criticised for yet another catastrophic stampede at the Hajj, a new bone of contention in its already frigid relations with Iran.

Saudi Arabia's human rights abuses are many and broad. Torture and ill-treatment are common, widespread and generally committed with impunity. The death penalty and corporal punishment are routinely ordered by the courts in criminal cases. Access to justice, fair trials and due process are denied, with many convictions based on confessions extracted under duress.

Discrimination against the Shia minority is rife. Migrant workers face serious abuse and are offered precious little government protection. Human rights defenders are harassed, detained and prevented from undertaking their work. Freedoms of expression, assembly and belief are regularly violated by law enforcement agencies and by government agents.

Storm in a teacup

Saudi Arabia also has an appalling record of discriminating against women. Using economic, political, education and health criteria, the World Economic Forum's *Gender Gap Index* in 2012 ranked Saudi Arabia 131 out of 135 countries.

The country's governorship system effectively means that women are unable to participate in society.

Somewhat perversely, Saudi Arabia is party to the Convention on the Elimination of All Forms of Discrimination against Women. The committee that monitors states' compliance with their obligations arising under that treaty has expressed grave concerns about Saudi women's rights.

Similar concerns have been raised by the Committee on the Rights of the Child, the Committee on the Elimination of Racial Discrimination and the Committee Against Torture. UN experts have spoken out against summary executions by firing squad and beheading. UN independent experts have also made recommendations on torture and ill-treatment, racism and xenophobia, arbitrary detention, and freedoms of belief and of expression within Saudi Arabia.

But of course, very little media attention is devoted to these issues until Saudi Arabia puts its head above the parapet, as it has on this latest case. And even then, lucrative international contracts aside, little can be done to effect significant change from afar.

Saudi Arabia is protected by its Gulf neighbours, and by its political allies within the Organisation of Islamic Co-operation. The country's oil reserves and wealth, its ties with the US, and its position among allied Muslim states mean that this latest media storm is very much confined to a teacup.

The cancelled British contract or the diplomatic fallout over Yemen and Syria are all very well, but the Saudi regime is still not being held to account for its gross and systemic violations of its citizens' human rights.

14 October 2015

⇨ The above information is reprinted with kind permission from *The Conversation*. Please visit www.theconversation.com for further information.

The treatment of Yazidi women highlights a historical issue: what makes someone human? THE CONVERSATION

An article from **The Conversation.**

By Simon Reich, Professor in the Division of Global Affairs and the Department of Political Science, Rutgers University Newark

The recent revelations about the savage treatment of Yazidi women at the hands of Islamic State, or ISIS, fighters is the latest in a shocking set of disclosures regarding the group's behaviour. It sadly echoes the abject treatment and sexual abuse reportedly suffered by Kayla Mueller, the American hostage who died in February while being held by ISIS.

For Americans, the disclosure is all the more uncomfortable because the reported trade in these women recalls many of the attributes of slavery as practised in the US until the American Civil War – a controversial comparison made by President Obama himself earlier in the year.

The horror of the systematically brutal treatment of these women cannot be rationalised by any religious philosophy. And it conforms to a general perception of radical Jihadism as a medieval one that defies conventional conceptions of what we like to call 'modernity.'

But the behaviour of ISIS raises a broader question: what does it mean to be 'human' in the modern world?

Being human

The answer may seem obvious to most of us. Being human is defined physically. It is being a member of a species.

Those with a more metaphysical approach might define it philosophically. As René Descartes said, "I think; therefore I am."

Others might focus on the legal aspects, as enshrined in the United Nations Declaration of Human Rights that was first proclaimed in 1948. It states that all humans have inalienable, fundamental human rights that must be protected.

But the sorry fact is that the definition of who is a human – and thus worthy of our concern – has always been contested and it still is today.

And the most important point is that this definition has had an enormous effect on when and where countries act to save lives; where and when they provide aid; and who is enslaved and abused.

The answer to these questions essentially distinguishes between who is human – and thus vulnerable and worthy of our protection and resources – and who is not.

Humanitarian intervention and gunboat diplomacy

Let's take the example of humanitarian intervention and civilian protection.

Over a decade ago, George Washington University political scientist Martha Finnemore wrote a short but highly informative book on the history of military intervention. In it she pointed out that the reasons that countries – or the international community as a whole – intervene has altered dramatically over time.

For example, the Europeans did so initially to collect sovereign debt in the early and mid-1800s – mostly from Latin America. They would sail in and seize any taxes that had been collected and stored in customs houses. That was a perfectly acceptable practice at the time. But imagine the gunboats sailing to Argentina today, a country that is officially bankrupt, to seize their money from bank vaults!

Indeed, the very idea of humanitarian intervention only developed later, and very selectively – initially to protect people 'like us'.

So, for example, a coalition force led by the Russian Empire invaded the Muslim Ottoman Empire in 1877 to protect orthodox Christian Slavs. Protecting your religious and ethnic brothers and sisters was acceptable. They were human. Others were not.

In fact, the universalising of the definition of the human to justify intervening where there is no ethnic or religious tie is a relatively recent idea.

It is one that has only really gained traction since the end of the Cold War.

As the United Nation's 'Responsibility to Protect' initiative makes crystal clear, when it come to humanitarian intervention to protect vulnerable populations, humanity isn't defined by religion, skin colour, gender, race or caste. But that initiative has taken off only in the last 15 years and the principle has been applied only on a very limited basis. The multilateral intervention against

Muammar Qaddafi's government in 2011 remains the most prominent example.

The principle and practice of sexual violence

Of course, addressing these issues in practice is always more complicated than in principle. And the issue of who is a human is still very much contested today – far more so than many of us might imagine.

Take the example of the inhumane treatment of the Yazidi women, held against their will, sold like chattels and sexually abused. It has all the hallmarks of slavery. Yet while an extreme example, it is by no means unique – either historically or in today's world.

Historically, we know that women have been enslaved and abused on a mass scale. The treatment of Korean 'Comfort Women' during the Second World War is an issue that still divides South Korea and Japan, as the self-immolation of a South Korean man on 12 August demonstrated. The same kind of sexual violence has been documented in numerous, more recent wars.

So it's not that sexual violence in war is a new problem. But it has become more documented and prominently discussed in policy circles in recent years.

The UN acknowledged, for example, that rape is a weapon of war and classified it as a war crime only in 2008.

This recognition is in large part explained by the fact that we have expanded our definition of the human – and thus become more aware of the issue.

21 million slaves... at least

Yet according to the *Global Slavery Index*, classifying certain people as not human is still a characteristic feature of many societies, particularly in Africa, Asia and the Middle East.

Modern slavery can take many forms: from using children as soldiers to men on fishing boats and women as industrial workers or as prostitutes. In each case it reduces a person to a commodity, denying them their essential humanity.

The United Nations estimates that there are upward of 21 million slaves in the world today, while the Global Slavery Index offers the larger figure of 35.8 million – the number changing depending on how they define a slave.

Sadly, these figures suggest that it is the reporting of the problem, rather than its scale, that has changed.

What is disturbingly clear from one major *New York Times* story is that a Yazidi can be given her freedom by her owner (albeit with ISIS' definition of the still limited rights of a Muslim woman) and thus 'become human.'

That's an idea so at odds with contemporary Western thinking it once again begs the question: if you are so opposed to it, what are you willing to do about it?

17 August 2015

⇨ The above information is reprinted with kind permission from *The Conversation*. Please visit www.theconversation.com for further information.

© 2010-2016, The Conversation Trust (UK)

New cultural festival to highlight human rights

By Phil Miller

A new Scottish arts festival has been launched, called Declaration, which will see leading writers, filmmakers, musicians and visual artists appearing alongside human rights campaigners and people working across health and social care.

Declaration will be held at the Centre for Contemporary Arts (CCA) in Glasgow from 3–6 March.

In its first year, Declaration will feature 30 events, including film screenings, performances, debates and workshops.

Each one is inspired by one of the 30 articles in the 1948 Universal Declaration of Human Rights.

Artists taking part include novelist Louise Welsh and architect Jude Barber; performance poets Jenny Lindsay and Rachel McCrum, Amal Azzudin of the Glasgow Girls and Kate Pickett, co-author of international best-seller *The Spirit Level*, among others.

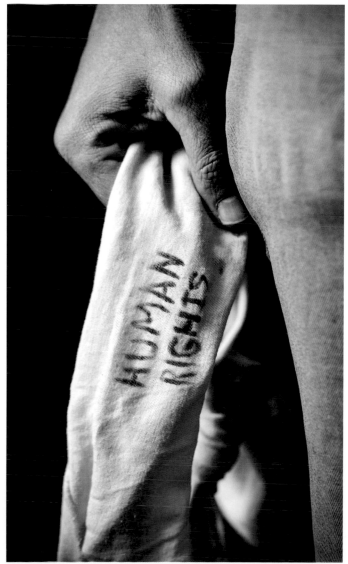

It will show a 50th anniversary screening of *Cathy Come Home*, director Ken Loach's influential 1966 TV play about homelessness.

> **"In its first year, Declaration will feature 30 events, including film screenings, performances, debates, and workshops"**

Louise Welsh and Jude Barber will revive their Empire Café project, which was part of the Glasgow Commonwealth Games cultural programme, exploring Glasgow's connection with the slave trade, with performance poet Dorothea Smartt.

There will be a pre-release preview screening of *The Divide*, the film version of best-selling book *The Spirit Level*, followed by a debate about the impact of inequality on health, well-being and prosperity with Joyce McMillan, Alex Massie, and *Spirit Level* co-author Kate Pickett.

There will be two separate performance events exploring the right to rest and leisure and the role they play in well being, and the right to a nationality, curated by Jenny Lindsay and Rachel McCrum of Rally & Broad, as well as a free screening of this year's Oscar-nominated documentary *He Named Me Malala*.

Lee Knifton, head of Mental Health Foundation in Scotland said: "We are very pleased to be working in partnership with NHS Health Scotland, the ALLIANCE and the University of Strathclyde to develop an exciting new festival which will explore the notion of health and human rights with the wider public and partners, creating new ideas and energy in this vital area."

Andrew Eaton-Lewis, Arts Lead for the Mental Health Foundation, said: "We're very excited to be announcing this festival programme. There's a huge variety of events on offer – all of them free – and we hope that people will want to spend a whole day, and perhaps a whole weekend, helping us to kick start a wider debate about what human rights mean today – and what impact it has on the health of individuals, and of a society, when people are denied those rights."

4 February 2016

⇨ The above information is reprinted with kind permission from *Herald Scotland*. Please visit www.heraldscotland.com for further information.

The foundation of international human rights law

The Universal Declaration of Human Rights is generally agreed to be the foundation of international human rights law. Adopted in 1948, the UDHR has inspired a rich body of legally binding international human rights treaties. It continues to be an inspiration to us all whether in addressing injustices, in times of conflicts, in societies suffering repression, and in our efforts towards achieving universal enjoyment of human rights.

It represents the universal recognition that basic rights and fundamental freedoms are inherent to all human beings, inalienable and equally applicable to everyone, and that every one of us is born free and equal in dignity and rights. Whatever our nationality, place of residence, gender, national or ethnic origin, colour, religion, language, or any other status, the international community on 10 December 1948 made a commitment to upholding dignity and justice for all of us.

Foundation for our common future

Over the years, the commitment has been translated into law, whether in the forms of treaties, customary international law, general principles, regional agreements and domestic law, through which human rights are expressed and guaranteed. Indeed, the UDHR has inspired more than 80 international human rights treaties and declarations, a great number of regional human rights conventions, domestic human rights bills, and constitutional provisions, which together constitute a comprehensive legally binding

system for the promotion and protection of human rights.

Building on the achievements of the UDHR, the International Covenant on Civil and Political Rights, and the International Covenant on Economic, Social and Cultural Rights entered into force in 1976. The two Covenants have developed most of the rights already enshrined in the UDHR, making them effectively binding on states that have ratified them. They set forth everyday rights such as the right to life, equality before the law, freedom of expression, the rights to work, social security and education. Together with the UDHR, the Covenants comprise the International Bill of Human Rights.

Over time, international human rights treaties have become more focused and specialised regarding both the issue addressed and the social groups identified as requiring protection. The body of international human rights law continues to grow, evolve, and further elaborate the fundamental rights and freedoms contained in the International Bill of Human Rights, addressing concerns such as racial discrimination, torture, enforced disappearances, disabilities, and the rights of women, children, migrants, minorities and indigenous peoples.

Universal values

The core principles of human rights first set out in the UDHR, such as universality, interdependence and indivisibility, equality and non-discrimination, and that human rights simultaneously entail both rights and obligations from duty bearers and rights owners, have been reiterated in numerous international human rights conventions, declarations and resolutions. Today, all United Nations member states have ratified at least one of the nine core international human rights treaties, and 80 per cent have ratified four or more, giving concrete expression to the universality of the UDHR and international human rights.

How does international law protect human rights?

International human rights law lays down obligations which States are bound to respect. By becoming parties to international treaties, states assume obligations and duties under international law to respect, to protect and to fulfil human rights. The obligation to respect means that states must refrain from interfering with or curtailing the enjoyment of human rights. The obligation to protect requires states to protect individuals and groups against human rights abuses. The obligation to fulfil means that States must take positive action to facilitate the enjoyment of basic human rights.

Through ratification of international human rights treaties, governments undertake to put into place domestic measures and legislation compatible with their treaty obligations and duties. The domestic legal system, therefore, provides the principal legal protection of human rights guaranteed under international law. Where domestic legal proceedings fail to address human rights abuses, mechanisms and procedures for individual and group complaints are available at the regional and international levels to help ensure that international human rights standards are indeed respected, implemented, and enforced at the local level.

⇨ From *The Foundation of International Human Rights Law*, by United Nations. © 2016 United Nations. Reprinted with the permission of the United Nations.

⇨ Visit www.un.org for further information.

European Convention on Human Rights

The European Convention on Human Rights (ECHR) is an international human rights treaty, which means an agreement between governments. It gives all people – adults, children and young people – a set of rights, such as the right to life and the right to freedom of religion.

The ECHR is divided into 'articles', or sections. Each article contains a different right. You can read about these below.

The Human Rights Act 1998 made the ECHR part of domestic law, which means that a person can take their case to court in England if they think their rights have been breached. If the English courts reject their claim, they can then take it to the European Court of Human Rights.

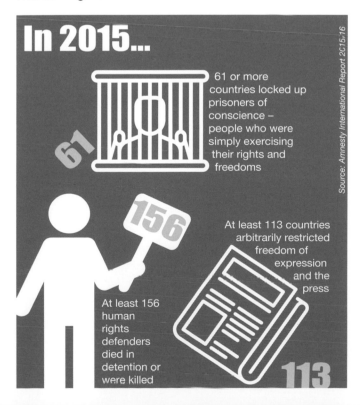

In 2015...

61 or more countries locked up prisoners of conscience – people who were simply exercising their rights and freedoms

At least 156 human rights defenders died in detention or were killed

At least 113 countries arbitrarily restricted freedom of expression and the press

Source: Amnesty International Report 2015/16

The rights in the ECHR are:

Article 2
The right to life.

Article 3
Freedom from torture and inhuman or degrading treatment or punishment.

Article 4
Freedom from slavery.

Article 5
Right to liberty and security.

Article 6
The right to a fair trial, including the child's right to be informed promptly, in a language he or she understands, of the alleged offence and to have an interpreter in court if he or she cannot understand or speak the language used in court. Restrictions on reporting can be applied to protect the interests of children.

Article 7
No one can be punished for an act that was not a criminal offence when it was carried out.

Article 8
The right to respect for private and family life, home and correspondence.

Article 9
The right to freedom of thought, conscience and religion.

Article 10
The right to freedom of expression.

Article 11
The right to freedom of assembly and association.

Article 12
Right to marry.

Article 13

Right to an effective remedy.

Plus Article 2 of the First Protocol (a later addition) – the right to education, which must conform with parents' religious and philosophical convictions.

These are all supported by Article 14, which says that all the rights in the Convention apply to all people without discrimination.

Articles 8 to 11 are qualified rights – they can be interfered with, but only for a good reason (like public safety, economic well-being or the protection of the rights of others), in accordance with the law generally and only so far as is necessary in the individual case.

Children's rights

The Grand Chamber of the European Court of Human Rights has stated that:

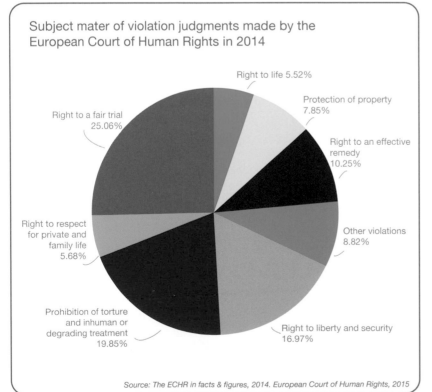

Subject mater of violation judgments made by the European Court of Human Rights in 2014

Right to life 5.52%

Protection of property 7.85%

Right to an effective remedy 10.25%

Right to a fair trial 25.06%

Other violations 8.82%

Right to respect for private and family life 5.68%

Right to liberty and security 16.97%

Prohibition of torture and inhuman or degrading treatment 19.85%

Source: The ECHR in facts & figures, 2014. European Court of Human Rights, 2015

The human rights of children and the standards to which all governments must aspire in realising these rights for all children are set out in The Convention on the Rights of the Child... The Convention spells out the basic human rights that children everywhere – without discrimination – have: the right to survival; to develop to the fullest; to protection from harmful influences, abuse and exploitation; and to participate fully in family, cultural and social life. It further protects children's rights by setting standards in health care, education and legal, civil and social services. States party to The Convention are obliged to develop and undertake all actions and policies in the light of the best interests of the child (Article 3). Moreover, States have to ensure that a child is not separated from his or her parents against their will unless such separation is necessary for the best interests of the child, and respect the right of a child who is separated from one or both parents to maintain personal relations and direct contact with both parents on a regular basis, except if it is contrary to the child's best interests (Article 9). (Sahin v Germany 2003).

⇨ The above information is reprinted with kind permission from CRAE. Please visit www.crae.org.uk for further information.

A guide to human rights legislation in the UK

Ever wondered what the difference is between the Human Rights Convention and the Human Rights Act? This may help.

By Joshua Rozenberg

Human rights will be a major issue in the forthcoming general election. The Labour party has just begun a political campaign, albeit one with remarkably ill-defined aims ("a Labour vision for human rights", "ensure they remain at the heart of Labour's policy and practice", and so on). The Conservatives recently sacked their well-respected attorney general, apparently because Dominic Grieve advised against the policy they are planning to announce at their party conference in October. And one of their justice ministers has said that Britain "should think of leaving the [human rights] convention if we can't get a satisfactory arrangement" with the court that enforces it.

Some people find the issues confusing. So what follows is a simplified guide. I have tried to make it objective, although I am sure readers will not hesitate to correct me if it is not.

What's the difference between the Human Rights Convention and the Human Rights Act?

The European Convention on Human Rights is a treaty: an international agreement. It was ratified by the United Kingdom in 1951 and entered into force in 1953. It has been signed by all 47 member states of the Council of Europe. The Human Rights Act was passed by the British Parliament in 1998 and entered into force two years later. It includes almost all the provisions, or 'articles', in the Convention, allowing judges to apply them in the courts of the United Kingdom.

Why is there an Act as well as a Convention?

To begin with, the Convention was not much use to individuals who wanted to complain that governments had not respected their human rights. Council of Europe member states did not agree to set up a human rights court until 1959. The British Government waited until 1966 before allowing individuals to bring cases against itself in the new court. And courts in the UK could not apply the Convention themselves until the Human Rights Act took effect in 2000. Until then, people seeking to enforce their human rights had to complain to the court in Strasbourg, a process that lasted years.

What does the Human Rights Act say?

There are two important provisions. The first says that other Acts of Parliament must be read and given effect in a way that is compatible with the Human Rights Convention, "so far as it is possible to do so". If it is not possible for senior judges to "read down" other legislation in this way, then all that the courts can do is to say so. The other important provision says that a UK court deciding a human rights case "must take into account" any relevant decision of the human rights court.

What happens if a court in the UK finds that other legislation is not compatible with the Convention?

It is for Parliament to decide whether to change the law. Special fast-track procedures are available. That is because it was thought that ministers would want to reform an incompatible law before the claimant could go to Strasbourg and defeat the Government.

What does "take into account" mean?

Many judges have expressed many opinions. Clearly, the statute does not make decisions of the human rights court binding on our own judges. But neither are they free to ignore Strasbourg decisions. Otherwise, a disappointed claimant would simply take a case to the human rights court and, again, the government would probably be defeated. Some people think that judges in Britain are too willing to go along with a court

The UK's human rights record
Outcome of judgments of, and application to, the European Court of Human Rights involving the United Kingdom, 2012–2014

The select few (results of judgments only)

29	21
UK win	UK loss

The bigger picture (results of applications*)

5,650	45
Inadmissible or struck out	36

*Multiple applications can be resolved in one judgment. In early 2015, over 1,000 applications were decided against the UK all at once, which would skew this chart.

Source: The Court and the UK in figures press release (Jan 2015); European Court of Human Rights UK country profile (Feb 2015); HUDOC database. Compiled by Full Fact

that is constantly reinterpreting and developing the convention as a 'living instrument'. But rewording the phrase "take into account" might not help a judge decide whether or not to follow a particular Strasbourg decision.

What would be the effect of repealing the Human Rights Act?

It depends whether Parliament puts anything in its place. If there is no replacement, then we are back to where we were before October 2000. People would be able to enforce their human rights, but they would have to go to Strasbourg to do so. That is the theory, anyway. In practice, I think that UK judges who have spent their judicial careers enforcing human rights would find ways of continuing to do so, perhaps by ruling that Convention rights such as privacy have now become part of the common law.

And what would happen if Parliament enacted a 'British' bill of rights?

If it contains rights that are based closely on the Convention, as currently interpreted by the human rights court, then we would be in the same position as we now are. But the more Convention rights that are missing from the new Act, the more cases would go to the Strasbourg and the more defeats the UK Government could expect to suffer.

What effect do those defeats have?

Article 46 of the Human Rights Convention says that the states "undertake to abide by the final judgment of the court in any case to which they are parties". That means their governments must seek a change in the law.

And what if they do not?

Enforcement is the responsibility of the Council of Europe's committee of ministers. That is made up of the member states, which operate through their ambassadors in Strasbourg. Ever since the human rights court confirmed in 2005 that the UK's blanket ban on voting by convicted prisoners was a breach of their human rights, the committee has monitored the UK's non-compliance with that ruling. In March, the committee again urged the Government to introduce legislation.

What if Britain simply refuses to abide by the court's judgment on prisoner votes?

There has been a tacit understanding for some years that the committee would not make much of a fuss before the next general election. If the next government fails to take action, the UK could, in theory, be forced out of the Council of Europe. But the UK has always implemented the court's decisions and nobody wants to provoke a crisis.

What options are open to a government that does not want to abide by a decision of the court?

Article 58 of the Convention allows a member state to "denounce" the treaty – which means to pull out of it. Six months' notice is required and denunciation does not release a country from its existing obligations. But it would be difficult to enforce those obligations once a state had left.

What would the political consequences be?

There can be little doubt that the UK would have to leave the Council of Europe if it pulls out of the convention. Although there is much more to the Council of Europe than human rights, no country can join the 47-member body without first agreeing to be bound by the Human Rights Convention.

But that's not the same as leaving the European Union?

The two bodies are separate, though often confused and are becoming more closely connected. No country can join the EU without first joining the Council of Europe. But whether the UK could stay in the EU after leaving the Council of Europe would presumably be a matter for all 28 EU member states to decide.

Are there other options for the UK short of pulling out?

People have talked about renegotiating the UK's membership. But it seems unlikely that the Council of Europe would give special privileges to one particular state. Other members might think it better for the Council of Europe to lose a country that values human rights rather than to dilute obligations that are respected by countries which do not.

Is there a compromise?

According to Lord Faulks, the Justice Minister, Conservatives want the court to be "far less intrusive in areas where we have a clear view expressed by Parliament as our sovereign body". And that is just what the court clearly tried to be earlier this month when it decided that prisoners who had been denied their right to vote would not be awarded compensation or even their legal costs, thus deterring further applications.

Is that enough for the Conservatives?

Apparently not. They argue that the human rights court should never have ruled on claims such as prisoner voting. These issues, they say, should be a matter for Parliament and the UK Supreme Court. Those bodies should be sovereign.

Aren't they already sovereign?

They are in the sense that I explained earlier: the UK courts need only take Strasbourg rulings into account; and they cannot use the Human Rights Act to overrule incompatible primary legislation. But they are not sovereign for so long as the UK is committed under international law to abide by judgments of the human rights court.

What about a democratic override?

In the UK – though not in some other democracies, such as the United States – the legislature always has the last word. Parliament can overrule – or override – decisions taken by any court. By contrast, the Human Rights Convention gives the court and the Council of Europe states the last word. Lord Judge, the former Lord Chief Justice, is one of many distinguished lawyers who argue that the human rights court has too much power.

So how would the Conservatives make Parliament supreme?

According to Dominic Grieve, "the proposal that seems to have been floating about is that a Conservative government should enact primary legislation to state that, while Britain would still adhere to the European Convention, no judgment of the European court of human rights could be implemented without Parliament having approved its implementation in some way".

Would that work?

As a matter of domestic law, it would be fine. But an Act of Parliament cannot override the UK's treaty obligations. Non-implementation of a ruling by the human rights court would continue to be a breach of international law while we remained part of the Convention.

Could the UK live with that breach?

It might damage Britain's international reputation and moral authority. Grieve says the ministerial code would have to be amended so that officials could draft legislation that would otherwise breach the UK's international legal obligations.

So it would be better to pull out of the Convention?

It would be more honest; though it would do political damage to the UK and the Convention itself.

But at least it would give the UK control of its own human rights laws?

No. We would remain signed up to by the EU's charter of fundamental rights. This can be used to trump other Acts of Parliament when the courts are interpreting legislation required by EU law. If the UK pulls out of the Human Rights Convention, Grieve fears that the EU court of justice in Luxembourg – nothing to do with the human rights court in Strasbourg – would expand its role, requiring the UK to comply with human rights judgments.

So we would have to leave the EU too?

Yes. If we want to be sure we can make our own decisions on human rights in future without any risk that they will be overturned by a foreign court, the way forward is clear: we shall have to leave the Council of Europe and the European Union.

1 September 2014

⇨ The above information is reprinted with kind permission from *The Guardian*. Please visit www.theguardian.com for further information.

Anders Breivik should not be denied human rights, says Utøya survivor Bjorn Ihler

Strong words from a survivor of the massacre.

By Sarah Ann Harris

A survivor of Anders Breivik's massacre on the island of Utøya has defended a legal decision that the mass murderer's human rights were being violated in prison.

Breivik was convicted of terrorism and mass murder and jailed for 21 years in 2012, after killing 77 people in attacks on two parts of Norway in 2011.

The Oslo district court ruled on Wednesday that his prison conditions breached the European Convention on Human Rights prohibiting inhuman and degrading treatment.

The verdict drew horrified reactions from many.

But speaking on BBC Radio 4's *Today* programme, massacre survivor Bjørn Ihler said that although Breivik had denied his victims humanity, that did not justify them doing the same to him.

He said: "I think it's an extremely balanced decision. I think it shows great strength from the court's side that they were able to see that there might be faults in the ways in which the Norwegian imprisonment system has treated Breivik.

"I think that shows just how firmly the Norwegian court believes in equality before the law also when facing our worst terrorist.

> **"I think it shows great strength from the court's side that they were able to see that there might be faults in the ways in which the Norwegian imprisonment system has treated Breivik"**

"I think at the end of the day, he deserves the same human rights as any other inmate and I don't think he poses a particularly much larger threat than any one of those who believe in many of the same things as him who today live outside of prison and speak their hateful messages freely.

"Of course, Breivik denied us all humanity and all human rights. But that does not ever make it right for us to deny him the same thing. If we do that, we follow the same logic as him I think."

Ihler survived after fleeing into the waters surrounding the island in an attempt to escape Breivik, who pretended to be a police officer before continuing to fire at his victims.

The killer narrowly missed Ihler, who was able to swim around a corner to safety.

Breivik's attacks shocked on Norway on July 22, 2011. After months of meticulous preparations, he set off a car bomb outside the government headquarters in Oslo, killing eight people and wounding dozens.

> **"In a four-page hand-written letter to penitentiary officials, Breivik described the prison where is being held as 'hell' and made a list of 12 demands to improve the 'torture-like' conditions he claimed he is being forced to live in"**

He then drove to Utøya island, where he opened fire on the annual summer camp of the left-wing Labour Party's youth wing. Breivik killed 69 people killed, most of them teenagers, before he surrendered to police.

In 2014 police rejected a lengthy complaint from Breivik, who claimed his treatment in jail – including the quality of his video games – amounted to "serious torture."

In a four-page hand-written letter to penitentiary officials, Breivik described the prison where is being held as "hell" and made a list of 12 demands to improve the "torture-like" conditions he claimed he is being forced to live in.

Breivik's requests included that the PlayStation 2 he has access to is replaced by a more recent PlayStation 3. He also requested a computer to replace his "worthless" typewriter.

He also requested a sofa to replace the "painful" chair in his cell and that his weekly allowance be doubled to £60.

"You've put me in hell ... and I won't manage to survive that long. You are killing me," he wrote.

21 April 2016

⇨ The above information is reprinted with kind permission from The Huffington Post UK. Please visit www.huffingtonpost.co.uk for further information.

Why Michael Gove hopes to reinvent existing human rights law

Home Affairs: the policy promise was inherited by Gove after the party's election triumph.

By Nigel Morris

Michael Gove has been Justice Secretary for less than nine months, but has set about the job with the same passion for reform that characterised his spell running England's schools.

Out have gone several schemes dreamt up by his predecessor Chris Grayling, including the farcical criminal courts charge and cuts to legal aid. In have come commitments to turn round failing jails, boost the rehabilitation of offenders and drag courts into the 21st century.

But a Justice Secretary in a hurry to get things done has run into particularly daunting problems in one crucial area of his portfolio: human rights legislation.

Denouncing the so-called human rights lobby by pointing to stories of terrorists and dangerous criminals securing perverse court victories is a sure-fire way of winning cheers at Tory conferences.

It prompted a populist promise to replace the Human Rights Act, which enshrined the European Convention of Human Rights in UK law, with a British Bill of Rights and assert the supremacy of domestic judges over the European Court of Human Rights in Strasbourg.

Work on scrapping the Act, which was blocked in the Coalition by the Liberal Democrats, was begun by Grayling, leading at one point to the suggestion – encouraged by the Home Secretary Theresa May – that Britain could leave the convention altogether.

The policy promise, reiterated in last year's Tory manifesto, was inherited by Gove after the party's election triumph. And then it got stuck in the ministerial in-tray, as a pledge to produce plans for cracking down on human rights excesses in the new Government's first 100 days came and went.

Part of his problem is the huge complexity and sensitivity of the move. Critics complain it could undermine the constitutional arrangements underpinning devolution, even requiring the rewriting of the Good Friday Agreement, cause conflict with other European countries and damage the UK's reputation for defending human rights.

This week, while Westminster's attention was focused on Britain's future with the EU (which has no connection to the Strasbourg court), some of Gove's route through the maze began to emerge.

He told a parliamentary committee that his proposals would be published "soon", and would strengthen protection from prosecution for British soldiers serving abroad and put added emphasis on the right to free speech.

> **"The Bill of Rights now looks likely to include provision for a constitutional court to shield the UK from EU legislation, enshrining the supremacy of domestic courts over Brussels politicians as well as Strasbourg judges"**

These are relatively minor changes but, in more significant disclosures, the Justice Secretary said that everything in the European Convention would be contained in the Bill of Rights and subject to European law.

The announcement raises the question of why the Government is even bothering with complicated legislation if it is effectively replicating existing laws.

Gove explained it was important to tackle the public "perception" that human rights legislation is inspired by Europe rather than Britain. It was not put to him that much of that perception has been created by his fellow Tories and their press allies. The drive for repeal of the Act is, of course, partly political with ministers under pressure to deliver on a key manifesto promise, although there now appears to be a cross-over with David Cameron's EU negotiations.

The Bill of Rights now looks likely to include provision for a constitutional court to shield the UK from EU legislation, enshrining the supremacy of domestic courts over Brussels politicians as well as Strasbourg judges.

This is still a live issue as Cameron attempts to sell his reform plans to EU leaders and the country. It is perhaps the most pertinent explanation of why Gove is playing a waiting game over human rights.

4 February 2016

⇨ The above information is reprinted with kind permission from *The Independent*. Please visit www.independent.co.uk for further information.

Eight reasons why the Human Rights Act makes the UK a better place

Back in December 2013, Chris Grayling said he believed that the European Court of Human Rights (ECHR) did not "make this country a better place". Presumably he thinks this about the Human Rights Act too given the government's pledge to scrap it and turn human rights into a privilege Parliament chooses to bestow on the few it deems 'worthy'.

We fundamentally disagree – here are eight reasons why the Human Rights Act makes the UK a much better place.

1. Making 'never again' a reality

In the aftermath of the devastation of two world wars, our human rights were enshrined in law to ensure that these atrocities would never be repeated. The UK was instrumental in establishing the ECHR to protect us from human rights abuses by our own governments.

The Human Rights Act then came into force in the UK in 2000, bringing most of the rights contained in the ECHR into UK law so that individuals could take their cases to domestic courts for British protection, instead of having to wait for the slow wheels of justice to turn at the overstretched European Court of Human Rights.

2. Protecting us at our most vulnerable

Mr and Mrs Driscoll had lived together for over 65 years. Unable to walk unaided, Mr Driscoll relied on his wife to help him move around. She was blind and relied on her husband as her eyes. When Mr Driscoll was moved into a residential care home, Mrs Driscoll wanted to move to the home with her husband but was told she didn't meet the criteria.

"We have never been separated in all our years and for it to happen now, when we need each other so much, is so upsetting. I am lost without him – we were a partnership."

Mrs Driscoll

This was a clear breach of the couple's right to a family life as protected by the Human Rights Act, and a public campaign was launched to encourage social services to think again. As a result, Mrs Driscoll's needs were re-assessed and the couple were reunited – setting a precedent for elderly couples to be kept together in the same care home.

In a perfect world, we would all treat each other with the respect and care every human being deserves. Sadly, this isn't a reality. It's usually the most vulnerable, particularly the elderly and the sick, who suffer the most. That's why the Human Rights Act places public authorities in the UK – including hospitals and social services – under an obligation to treat everyone with fairness, equality and dignity.

3. Protecting women from domestic violence and keeping their families together

The obligations in the Human Rights Act helped a woman and her children find a safe home after leaving an abusive husband. Her husband had kept tracking them down, forcing them to move again and again.

When she arrived in London, the local social services department told her she was an unfit parent because she was making the family intentionally homeless by moving without justification and her children would be taken into foster care. With help from an advice worker, she argued the department was violating her rights under the Human Rights Act. At that point, they agreed – and the family stayed together.

4. Making it safer to be gay

Today, being gay could get you arrested or even executed in at least 78 countries. Thanks in large part to the ECHR and the Human Rights Act in the UK, our rights to be treated as equals with equal access to protection regardless of gender, sexuality, race or age are protected by law. The fight for equal rights has been significantly advanced by the laws.

Right up until 1982, 'male homosexual acts' were a crime in Northern Ireland. It was finally decriminalised following a human rights case brought forward by Jeff Dudgeon, a gay rights activist from Belfast.

In another landmark case in 2000, the Army was found to have violated the rights of two British

servicemen by dismissing them for being gay. This momentous case led to a change in UK law to allow gay members of the armed forces to be open about their sexuality.

5. Confirming that innocent means innocent

In 2008, the European Court of Human Rights ruled that the UK was violating an individual's right to privacy by holding fingerprint and DNA information of people who hadn't been charged or convicted of a crime – they said retaining the information "could not be regarded as necessary in a democratic society".

At the time, nearly one million innocent people had their DNA or fingerprints on the database, a fifth of the total database. As it swelled so did the concern that police were building a database of 'presumed guilt'. Beforehand, the UK Law Lords had defended the police's right to hold our personal information in this way – it took a European Court judgement for common sense to prevail.

6. Helping us challenge these injustices in the UK courts

Introducing the Human Rights Act meant that UK courts could look at the ECHR and judge whether the authorities were respecting the rights it protected. More than that, it requires public authorities to ensure their decisions and actions do not violate rights, so there is far less need to go to court to get protection.

Before that, for over 20 years, the only way to challenge that was at the European Court of Human Rights. The Human Rights Act brought our rights home, and countless everyday decisions, like the domestic violence case above, making the UK better without a costly court process.

7. ...and challenge that decision at a higher court

That human rights are for all of us – the best and the worst – was the aim of the politicians like Churchill and Roosevelt when the Universal

Declaration of Human Rights was created, and the European Convention and the European Court are direct descendants of that. Having the European Court of Human Rights ensures that human rights are applied consistently in 47 countries.

The only country in Europe not in the ECHR is Belarus, Europe's last dictatorship. Even Russia and Azerbaijan – countries with less than stellar human rights records – are part of the Convention. Even then, the ECHR doesn't set law in any of these 47 countries. It makes a judgement when something is 'incompatible' with our protected human rights, and lets the government in question decide how to fix the incompatibility.

In the case of the DNA database, the UK Government put time limits in places so DNA of those not charged or convicted is held for just six years – balancing our right to privacy with the responsibilities of the state to tackle crime.

8. Allowing the UK to take a stand for human rights everywhere

We're rightly proud of our tough stance around the world on human rights. The UK will not extradite to

a country where the death penalty is used. UK politicians have called for Guantanamo to be closed and laws criminalising homosexuality in Africa and elsewhere to be overturned.

What happens when we remove ourselves from the court and laws that protect our rights in the UK? Will our attempts to end female genital mutilation or ensure women's rights lead to a polite refusal from the country in question?

We can't make the world a better place if we turn our back on human rights, and European Convention and Court that we helped put into place to make everyone's lives better.

10 February 2016

⇨ The above information is reprinted with kind permission from Amnesty International. Please visit www.amnesty.org.uk for further information.

© Amnesty International 2016

Magna Britain – a British Bill for human rights

By David Atehortua

At the end of March (2015), the Government's human rights watchdog sent an open letter to Britain's Joint Committee on Human Rights, expressing worries with the Conservative proposal to repeal the Human Rights Act and replace it with a British Bill of Rights and Responsibilities.

The letter recognises there is a concern about the interpretation of human rights law, and suggests that "any changes to the current framework might offer an opportunity to bring additional rights". However, the overall tone of the letter suggests disbelief in the proposal and stresses their "regressive" nature, including the potential broader constitutional consequences such proposals would mean for Britain. The letter concludes, saying, "We must safeguard our reputation for fairness and our moral authority when confronting human rights abuses abroad."

The Conservative proposals have gained some support.

The media, senior British judges and public opinion favour a British Bill of Rights. A YouGov poll in 2014 asked the question, should Britain withdraw from the European Convention on Human Rights (ECHR)? 41% answered yes (down from 48% the year before) and 38% answered no. But given the vast majority of people do not realise that the ECHR has nothing to do with the EU, hostility to the Convention may in fact be little more than a general suspicion of all things European.

One of the strongest endorsements for a new Bill came from the former Lord Chief Justice, Lord Judge, who argues that the "living instrument" nature of the convention is "undermining democracy".

We are now in a situation where Britain's legally enforceable principles come from a foreign, unaccountable court, and not from our own democratically-elected Parliament. This is particularly worrying because the consequences of this judicial-political ambiguity is unchartered territory and a disaster waiting to happen if we fail to return human rights law to its original noble purpose.

Why should we be relying on judicial practice and presumptive meaning to become our morally acceptable principles and manifest in our laws, when this is fundamentally the role of Parliament? Whatever happened to democracy? The rule of law is not the same as rule by courts and lawyers. It is the responsibility of the judiciary to restrict their decisions to what the law says, and not to make up new laws, as is the case now in Strasbourg.

Hence it is of vital importance for the future of Britain that we do not look at the European Convention of Human Rights as the end point of human rights, but that instead we challenge it and improve it.

A British Bill of Rights would certainly challenge it, but as to whether it would improve it very much depends on what the Bill contains.

If, as has been suggested, the final proposal revealed by the Conservatives limits the British Bill of Rights to merely an uninspiring replica of the original Convention with a similar wording, it would be a real shame and a wasted opportunity to create, once again, a charter of human rights law that every other country would want to follow.

A convincing bill should add some rights, balance the existing ones, and include civic duties. Some suggestions from experts as to what should be added to the Bill include:

- ⇨ The right to a jury trial. This is still a cornerstone of British justice, despite Labour's best efforts in 2005 to scrap it for some cases. A right many European countries do not have, and one that could be added to the British Bill of Rights.

- ⇨ The limited right to reputation. A better balance needs to be struck between privacy and reputation on the one hand, and freedom of speech on the other. These ideas are in tension with each other and neither is absolutely protected by the law, a new human rights framework could give freedom of speech, under specific circumstances, primacy over privacy.

- ⇨ Ratify the Geneva Conventions as the only law for war-like operations. A recent report by Policy Exchange highlights how "requiring soldiers on the battlefield to operate to the same standard as police officers patrolling the streets of London will make future overseas combat operations impossible".

- ⇨ Adopt guiding principles on business human rights responsibilities. This notion has already made progress at the UN. As companies become bigger than states, transcending (and occasionally trespassing on) territories and jurisdictions, we must guarantee they respect human rights throughout their operations. The responsibility for the protection of human rights should not only lie on the state's shoulders, but also on such corporations, which can contribute to a socially sustainable globalisation.

Finally, the biggest challenge to this policy may not come from international politics but from Scotland and Northern Ireland.

SNP ministers have said they would resist the withdrawal from the ECHR – the ECHR was written into the Scottish devolution settlement. The last thing this Government should do is to give the SNP opportunities to present themselves as a "liberal, open minded group protecting Scotland from an authoritarian and bigoted UK Government".

For its part, the Good Friday agreement, signed at the end of Northern Ireland's conflict, made the recognition of European human rights law a fundamental part of negotiations. Northern Ireland's committee on the administration of justice has warned that repealing the Human Rights Act "would shatter confidence within communities over politically sensitive policing reforms".

There is much at stake here. The Conservative party needs a demonstrably better plan if it wants to successfully sail these rough seas, otherwise the reputation of the UK over human rights will take a pounding.

11 April 2015

⇨ This piece was first published in the 2015 on The Bow Group website and is reprinted with kind permission from The Bow Group. Please visit www.bowgroup.org for further information.

Crucial new anti-slavery powers come into force

By James Mildred

Key parts of the UK Government's landmark modern slavery legislation come into force across England and Wales today, meaning offenders will face much tougher sentences when caught.

The Modern Slavery Act, given Royal Assent by the Queen in March this year, is the first dedicated piece of anti-slavery legislation across England and Wales for nearly 200 years.

Under the Act, the maximum custodial sentence for offenders rises from 14 years to life imprisonment.

Reparation orders also come into force to encourage courts to seize assets from perpetrators to help compensate victims.

Victims are also afforded stronger protection from prosecution for crimes committed when trapped in slavery and will now have access to civil legal aid.

Leading Christian charity CARE campaigned heavily for anti-slavery legislation for a number of years and the charity's spokesman has welcomed today as a significant moment in the fight against modern slavery.

CARE spokesman James Mildred said:

"This is a day of huge significance in the fight against modern slavery.

"The legacy of Wilberforce thankfully still lingers across our nation, but his stand against slavery was made hundreds of years ago.

"Today, this generation has taken a step in combating the scourge of 21st-century slavery.

"Thousands of exploited people are trapped in slavery in the UK according to Home Office estimates and their plight could not be ignored which is why CARE championed the need for dedicated anti-slavery legislation and worked closely with other charities to encourage the Government to take action.

"Thanks to the landmark Modern Slavery Act, action is now being taken to empower victims and bring offenders to justice."

31 July 2015

⇨ The above information is reprinted with kind permission from CARE. Please visit www.care.org.uk for further information.

UN Convention on the Rights of the Child

The UN Convention on the Rights of the Child (UNCRC) is an international treaty – an agreement between different countries – designed specifically to meet the needs of children. Children have all of the rights in other international human rights treaties too, but the UNCRC includes additional rights which only children need.

The UNCRC says that all children and young people under the age of 18 have certain rights. The Convention is separated into 54 'articles', or sections. The rights in the treaty include the right to education, the right to play, the right to health and the right to respect for privacy and family life. You can read about the rights protected by the Convention here.

All children should enjoy all of the rights, without discrimination on grounds such as disability, sex, race, age or sexual orientation, and whatever the circumstances in which they live or are cared for.

When a state ratifies (signs up to) a treaty it takes on legal obligations under international law. The UK ratified the UNCRC in December 1991. Unfortunately the Convention has not been made part of our domestic law, meaning that a child cannot go to court relying only on the UNCRC. However, as international law, the Convention is meant to be followed and should be referred to by courts, tribunals and other administrative processes when making decisions that affect children. Public bodies should also comply with it. This means that the UNCRC can be referred to in courts, tribunals and administrative proceedings such as case conferences, reviews and school exclusion panels.

The UN Committee on the Rights of the Child (the Committee) is a group of 18 children's rights experts from different countries. It meets three times a year in Geneva.

It has three main roles:

⇨ Every five years the Committee makes recommendations to governments, called Concluding Observations, telling them how to improve the protection of children's rights.

⇨ The Committee can hear complaints from individual children who think that their rights have been breached. Children can only take a case to the Committee if their Government has signed up to the 'individual complaints mechanism'. The UK Government has not done this yet, but CRAE is asking for it to do so.

⇨ The Committee explains what the rights in the UNCRC mean in more detail in 'General Comments'. You can find these at www.crae.org.uk.

⇨ The above information is reprinted with kind permission from CRAE. Please visit www.crae.org.uk for further information.

© CRAE 2016

We have an opportunity to create a new 'common sense' on human rights

By Rachel Krys, Communications Director, Equally Ours

Children are experiencing human rights abuses every day in the UK. Child abuse and neglect, lack of adequate housing and inadequate provision of specialist services for particular groups like children in care, care leavers and disabled children. More than ever, children need their human rights to be made a reality.

Across the country, children and their advocates use human rights to achieve real change and force authorities to make their policies and practices fairer. Human rights meant that a local authority was prosecuted for failing four children who were suffering neglect and abuse at the hands of their parents. Three teenage brothers were able to use human rights to argue they should have access to a lawyer to represent their views in court about which parent should have custody. A homeless family won the right to stay together after a judge ruled the council, which initially planned to take the children away from their mother, had failed to do a proper human rights assessment of their situation. Hughes used human rights to change the law around how young people are treated by the police after he was arrested and kept in a cell without his mother, or any appropriate adult, being informed.

These cases are at the heart of what children's organisations do, so why aren't we all talking about human rights?

It could be that human rights feel like a hard sell at the moment. The way rights are talked about in the media makes telling a positive story seem impossible. And it will take more than a few words or slogans to influence unconvinced people that human rights are worth defending. But there is too much to lose, and in fact it is possible to make a positive case for human rights, build public support and connect human rights to the values and freedoms most of us already care about.

In 2014, Equally Ours carried out audience research to identify ways to communicate a range of equality and social justice issues using human rights frames. Through a survey of 2,500 people from all over the UK, we tested over 30 messages linking equality and social justice issues with human rights. A large group, 40% of the population as a whole, are conflicted about human rights – they think human rights may be a good thing in theory, but they are heavily influenced by the negative media discourse. When we presented this group with messages that make rights relevant to their lives we saw that they not only agreed with the content of the messages but also became more positive about human rights in general.

The results show that making the link between equality and social justice issues and human rights works well – both for the issue AND for human rights. Importantly, of the messages we tested, some of those that focus on children's issues were particularly effective. For example:

"Children have the human right to a childhood free from poverty. That means sometimes we need the state to help make sure that every child has enough to eat, proper clothing and a safe warm home.": This message not only had 79% agreement but was also very effective in making people feel more positively about human rights generally.

"All children have a basic human right to a childhood free from abuse and neglect. We all have a responsibility to do more to protect this right in practice": 84% of people in our undecided cluster agreed with this statement, which frames abuse and neglect as human rights issues.

"When two young brothers, who were in the care of the local authority, were abused in a children's home, their calls for help were repeatedly ignored. It's important that we have human rights laws that helped them to challenge the system and get the help they needed." This message about the looked-after brothers is long, with a lot of detail on a subject which is not an everyday experience for most people. However, 85% of people agreed that it is important we have human rights laws to protect children in this situation. This shows that it is possible to weave human rights messages into statements without switching people off.

What does this mean for the way we could talk about human rights? When highly trusted charities and organisations use these tested messages about human rights in their work it has real impact with the public.

Age UK, for example, has been campaigning on behalf of older people who face abuse in care homes. This year, they released a short film, *Charles' Story*, which powerfully highlights links between dignity, respect and human rights. The film was designed to evoke intrinsic values and an emotional viewer response, resulting in positive feelings about human rights. At the time of writing, Charles' Story had reached over a million people with more than 300,000 unique views. For many, this could be their first exposure to a positive take on human rights.

Women's Aid launched a film targeting football fans and their clubs. *Unpunished* uses football imagery and metaphors to address domestic violence. Again, the strategy was to introduce human rights to a new audience in an unexpected context. These films do not educate about the details of human rights; rather, they connect issues the viewer already cares about with 'human rights', perhaps for the first time.

This shows it could be possible for children's organisations to carefully weave messages about human rights into conversations about their work.

So, as a starting point, children's organisations making and talking about the connections between human rights protections and children's experiences of abuse, poverty, crime and children's services could make people feel more positive about human rights and build support for social justice and equality more widely. Messages which make human rights relevant to people's everyday lives are the most helpful. This can be as simple as using inclusive words and phrases that focus on human rights as something that 'we' can be proud of or 'we' should support.

Equally Ours has started to collect stories – including about children – which make these connections as a resource to help organisations communicate how human rights affect the people they support. This growing databank of human rights stories can be found on our website: www.equally-ours.org.uk/human-rights-stories.

In light of the Government's anticipated plans to scale back our human rights laws, there is an opportunity to create a new 'common sense' on human rights. If children's organisations started to weave positive messages about human rights into their work, it would shift the current, negative terms of the debate and help build consensus that human rights are for everyone. Reframed as positive and relevant, human rights can then continue to be used by children's organisations as a tool to ensure that all children in the UK have the best possible start in life.

Equally Ours is an initiative that aims to change the conversation on human rights by inspiring people to understand how they benefit all of us in very practical ways. We work with charities and voluntary organisations to share stories of how human rights matter to the people they support in the UK. Visit www.equally-ours.org.uk and, to find out more and get involved, email Rachel.Krys@equally-ours.org.uk and Anna.Edmundson@equally-ours.org.uk.

⇨ The above information is reprinted with kind permission from Children England. Please visit www.childrenengland.org.uk for further information.

Key facts

- In 1948, in the aftermath of the Second World War, the newly formed United Nations adopted the Universal Declaration of Human Rights (UDHR). (page 1)

- In 2015, 122 or more countries tortured or otherwise ill-treated people. (page 2)

- 30 or more countries illegally forced refugees to return to countries where they would be in danger. (page 2)

- In the UK each year about 2,000 men, women and children are helped to escape from trafficking, but this is just the tip of the iceberg. The Government estimates there are 10,000 – 13,000 victims of modern slavery in the UK. (page 3)

- The 2014 *Global Report on Trafficking in Persons* released in Vienna and in various UNODC field office locations across the world shows that one in three known victims of human trafficking is a child – a five per cent increase compared to the 2007–2010 period. Girls make up two out of every three child victims, and together with women, account for 70 per cent of overall trafficking victims worldwide. (page 7)

- The vast majority of convicted traffickers – 72 per cent – are male and citizens of the country in which they operate. (page 7)

- There are over 21 million children, women and men living in modern slavery, three out of every 1,000 people worldwide. If they all lived together in a single city, it would be one of the biggest cities in the world. (page 9)

- There are over 1.5 million people working in slavery-like conditions in Europe, North America, Japan and Australia. (page 9)

- A recent ILO study estimated that modern slavery generates annual profits of over US$150 billion, which is as much as the combined profits of the four most profitable companies in the world. (page 9)

- Each year, 15 million girls are married before the age of 18. That is 28 girls every minute. (page 10)

- More than 700 million women alive today were married before their 18th birthday. That is the equivalent of 10% of the world's population. (page 10)

- Most adolescent pregnancies (90%) take place within marriage. (page 10)

- More than 1,000 cases of female genital mutilation (FGM) were recorded in just three months in the UK, it has been revealed. (page 12)

- Last year, the Government's Forced Marriage Unit provided support and assistance for 1,267 possible cases of forced marriage. (page 15)

- In the year since forced marriage was criminalised in the UK, only one conviction has taken place. In June, a 34-year-old man was jailed for forcing a 25-year-old woman to marry him under duress. (page 15)

- Since 1984, 155 states have ratified the UN Convention Against Torture, 142 of which are researched by Amnesty International. In 2014, Amnesty International observed at least 79 of these still torturing. (page 17)

- The vast majority (82%) believe there should be clear laws against torture. However, more than a third (36%) still think torture could be justified in certain circumstances. (page 17)

- More than 125 million women and girls in 29 countries in Africa and the Middle East have experienced Female Genital Mutilation or Cutting (FGM/C). (page 19)

- In 2015, 61 or more countries locked up prisoners of conscience – people who were simply exercising their rights and freedoms. (page 27)

- At least 113 countries arbitrarily restricted freedom of expression and the press in 2015. (page 27)

- Anders Breivik was convicted of terrorism and mass murder and jailed for 21 years in 2012, after killing 77 people in attacks on two parts of Norway in 2011. (page 32)

- The UNCRC says that all children and young people under the age of 18 have certain rights. The Convention is separated into 54 'articles', or sections. The rights in the treaty include the right to education, the right to play, the right to health and the right to respect for privacy and family life. (page 38)

Child marriage

Where children, often before they have reached puberty, are given to be married – often to a person many years older.

Domestic servitude

A type of labour trafficking. Domestic workers perform household tasks such as child-care, cleaning, laundry and cooking.

European Convention on Human Rights

An international treaty that protects the human rights and freedoms of people in Europe.

Female genital mutilation (FGM)

FGM is a non-medical cultural practice that involves partially or totally removing a girl or woman's external genitalia.

Forced labour

When someone is forced to work, or provide services, against their will. This is often the result of a person being trafficked into another country and then having their passport withheld, or threats made against their family.

Forced marriage

A marriage that takes place without the consent of one or both parties. Forced marriage is not the same as arranged marriage, which is organised by family or friends but which both parties freely enter into.

Human Rights

The basic rights all human beings are entitled to, regardless of who they are, where they live or what they do. Concepts of human rights have been present throughout history, but our modern understanding of the term emerged as a response to the horrific events of the Holocaust. While some human rights, such as the right not to be tortured, are absolute, others can be limited in certain circumstances: for example, someone can have their right to free expression limited if it is found they are guilty of inciting racial hatred.

Human trafficking

The transport and/or trade of people from one area to another, usually for the purpose of forcing them into labour or prostitution.

Human Rights Act

The Human Rights Act is a written law (statute) passed in 1998 which is in force in England and Wales. The rights that are protected by this law are based on the articles of the European Convention on Human Rights. There is an ongoing debate between supporters of the Act and its critics as to whether it should be kept, or replaced with a new UK Bill of Rights.

Organ harvesting

In relation to people-trafficking, organ harvesting occurs when a person is trafficked into the country by people who's intention is to remove one or more of their organs and sell them on the black-market.

Slavery

A slave is someone who is denied their freedom, forced to work without pay and considered to be literally someone else's property. Although slavery is officially banned internationally, there are an estimated 27 million slaves worldwide. Article 4 of the Universal Declaration of Human Rights states that 'No one shall be held in slavery or servitude; slavery and the slave trade shall be prohibited in all their forms'.

Torture

Intentionally causing a person physical or mental pain or suffering in order to obtain information or force them to make a confession. Under Article 5 of the Universal Declaration of Human Rights, 'No one shall be subjected to torture or to cruel, inhuman or degrading treatment or punishment'. The subject of torture, and whether it might be considered a necessary evil in the war against terror, has recently been the subject of controversy.

Universal Declaration of Human Rights

The first international, secular agreement on what were formerly called 'the rights of man', which arose from the desire of the world's governments to prevent the recurrence of the atrocities of the Second World War by setting out a shared bill of rights for all peoples and all nations. The text is non-binding, but it retains its force as the primary authority on human rights, and has been supported by the UN's ongoing work to encourage its incorporation into domestic laws.

United Nations Convention on the Rights of the Child (UNCRC)

An international human rights treaty that protects the rights of all children and young people under 18. The UK signed the convention on 19 April 1990 and ratified it on 16 December 1991. When a country ratifies the convention it agrees to do everything it can to implement it. Every country in the world has signed the convention except the USA and Somalia.

Yazidi

An ethnically Kurdish religious community originating from Mesopotamia. They live mainly in the Nineveh Province of Iraq.

Assignments

Brainstorming

⇨ In small groups, discuss what you know about human rights. Consider the following:

- What are human rights?

- What is the Human Rights Act?

- What is human trafficking?

Research

⇨ Research the issue of human trafficking and write a report about its prevalence in the UK.

⇨ Choose one of the types of human trafficking listed in the article on page 4 and research it further. With a partner, who has researched a different type of trafficking, share your findings.

⇨ Create a graph that illustrates the contents of the table on page 8. You can use more than one graph if necessary. Think carefully about the kind of graph you need to use.

⇨ Choose one of the countries from the graph of the highest rates of child marriage on page 11. Research child marriage in that country and feedback to your class.

⇨ Read the article *Cancelled UK deal won't change Saudi Arabia's appalling human rights record* on page 22 and do some research to find out exactly what the author means by the term 'human rights record'. Why is Saudi Arabia's record appalling? Write some notes and feedback to your class.

Design

⇨ Design a booklet to explain the content and scope of the Human Rights Act 1998. Include a timeline demonstrating its history and its links to the Universal Declaration of Human Rights.

⇨ Design a poster that highlights one particular type of human trafficking e.g. child trafficking, forced labour, etc.

⇨ Choose an article from this book and create an illustration to accompany it.

⇨ In small groups, design a campaign that will highlight the issue of child marriage. Your campaign could take electronic, video or printed form. Include samples of your campaign material and a written plan of at least 500 words explaining your thinking behind the campaign.

⇨ Imagine you work for a charity that is organising a festival of human rights. In groups of three or four, plan your festival. Will it be a one-day event, or will people camp overnight? What kinds of activities will take place? How will you ensure the festival is fun and attractive to visitors, while getting across important messages about human rights issues? Will you have guest speakers at your festival? Who might these be? You should create a written plan to explain these points, and could also include illustrations if you wish.

⇨ Create your own, easy-to-read version of the guide to human rights law on page 29.

Oral

⇨ In pairs, create a PowerPoint presentation that explores the indicators of human trafficking. Include a section that advises people what they should do if they suspect someone has been 'trafficked'.

⇨ Divide your class into two halves. One half should argue for a British Bill of Rights, and the other half should argue against it.

⇨ Choose an article from the *European Convention on Human Rights* (page 27) and, in pairs or small groups, discuss how your life might change if this right was taken away.

⇨ In pairs, discuss whether you think criminal Anders Breivik should be treated differently from other offenders.

Reading/writing

⇨ Write your own Bill of Rights for the UK. What rights do you think should be enshrined in law? Would all rights be absolute, or could some be limited in certain circumstances? What stipulations and provisos would you want to include with your list of rights?

⇨ Read the book *Nineteen Eighty-Four* by George Orwell, set in a future dystopia in which the right to free expression is controlled by the nightmarish 'Big Brother'. Write a review. Do you think Orwell saw his book as a warning?

⇨ Write an article for your school newspaper that explores the issue of forced marriage.

⇨ Read *Amnesty International Annual Report 2014/15* (pages 20–21) and write a summary that highlights the key issues raised.

⇨ Imagine that you live in a future society where you no longer have the right to 'freedom of thought'. Write a short-story or a fictional diary entry that illustrates what your life might be like.

Acknowledgements

The publisher is grateful for permission to reproduce the material in this book. While every care has been taken to trace and acknowledge copyright, the publisher tenders its apology for any accidental infringement or where copyright has proved untraceable. The publisher would be pleased to come to a suitable arrangement in any such case with the rightful owner.

Images

All images courtesy of iStock except page 12: Pixabay, page 26: MorgueFile, page 28 © Rock Cohen and page 34: Michael Ash.

Icons on pages 2 and 27 made by Freepik from www.flaticon.com

Illustrations

Don Hatcher: pages 4 & 17. Simon Kneebone: pages 14 & 35. Angelo Madrid: pages 10 & 22.

Additional acknowledgements

Editorial on behalf of Independence Educational Publishers by Cara Acred.

With thanks to the Independence team: Mary Chapman, Sandra Dennis, Christina Hughes, Jackie Staines and Jan Sunderland.

Cara Acred

Cambridge

May 2016